# THE MEGHAN FACTOR

## A ROYAL EXPERT'S INSIGHT ON AMERICA'S NEW PRINCESS—AND HOW SHE COULD CHANGE THE WINDSOR DYNASTY FOREVER

PATRICK JEPHSON

A BOMBARDIER BOOKS BOOK
An Imprint of Post Hill Press

ISBN: 978-1-64293-036-8
ISBN (eBook): 978-1-64293-037-5

The Meghan Factor:
A Royal Expert's Insight on America's New Princess—and How She Could Change the Windsor Dynasty Forever


Cover Design by Cody Corcoran

Post Hill Press, LLC
New York • Nashville
posthillpress.com

Published in the United States of America

*For*

*MARY JO*

*With love and thanks*

# Contents

Prologue........................................................... 5

In the Shadow of Diana............................................ 11

Meghan—Your Endless Audition Starts Here........... 29

Golden Twilight—Elizabeth's Long Autumn ............ 45

Charles—and the Many Faces of Duty .................... 57

William and Catherine and Harry…and Meghan .... 69

Harry—Handle with Care ........................................ 85

"The Fab Four"—More than a Tribute Band ............ 99

The Meghan Factor Meets the Majesty Factor ........ 125

Epilogue........................................................... 141

About the Author.................................................. 143

# Prologue

Do you want to be a British princess?

Meghan Markle of California, USA, has said that she does. Or, more romantically—and surely more accurately—she has said "Yes" to marrying Prince Harry, with the princess bit being very much a secondary part of the deal. That is the proper order of priorities, after all.

However, there's no getting away from it: a marriage that doesn't just start a new life but also takes her into the heart of the House of Windsor is going to give Meghan a steep learning curve—much steeper than some of the other options that might have been open to her.

And in its turn, the British Royal Family may have to do some adapting to the newcomer, even though that's not a regular habit. It's more than eighty years since the last American attached herself to its exclusive family tree—and that ended badly. Wallis Simpson's marriage to King Edward VIII in 1936 cost him his throne and earned him a lifetime of exile. The constitutional trauma of what became known as the Abdication Crisis left deep scars in the country and in the family, whose members have famously long memories.

Things had better be different this time around.

But will they?

♛♛♛

In this book, longtime royal insider and bestselling author Patrick Jephson draws upon his unique experience as Princess Diana's first (and only) private secretary/chief of staff to give an expert assessment of the momentous marital gamble the House of Windsor is about to take.

As a naturalized American citizen, he brings a special insight to the transatlantic dimension the new princess adds to the royal line-up. He's also able to analyze with a practiced eye the challenges faced by Meghan as she transitions to life in a palace—and the impact she'll have on the world's most famous monarchy.

Meghan's arrival could be a well-timed boost for a dynasty that faces big challenges in the coming years. But he doesn't skip the hard reality that survival as a royal newcomer takes more than a winning smile and a stylish curtsy. Meghan is committing to a path of duty and sacrifice that will last to the end of her days. Happily, with Prince Harry at her side, there's every chance of fun and fulfillment along the way—and a legacy that leaves her very personal mark on the House of Windsor forever.

Like Wallis, Meghan is a divorcee and already a mature woman with a lifetime's worth of valuable experience to her name. Also like Wallis, she's slim, brunette, and something of a fashion plate.

Luckily, the similarities between the women seem to end there. Nor are there many similarities between the royal world of today and the court of the 1930s. Modern princes are free to marry—and re-marry—pretty much as they please, perhaps in hopes of improving the odds of long-term marital success. The statistics for top-level royal marriages during Queen Elizabeth's reign are enough to make any potential royal bride think twice:

out of six starters, only two are still running: Edward and William, unlike divorcees Margaret, Anne, Andrew, and Charles.

Meghan may quite rightly have decided that she and Harry need fear nothing from the past in making their own marriage a beacon of stability, longevity, and happiness. But there are plenty of good examples from recent royal history that could give her some valuable tips for success—and quite a few cautionary tales too.

Forget Wallis Simpson. The real point of comparison is a much more familiar figure: Harry's much-missed mother. Meghan has already attracted hundreds of comparisons with Princess Diana, an iconic figure who will probably be a frequent presence throughout Meghan's princess career.

Diana's example of how to use the royal cachet to benefit good causes is one her sons are already following to universal praise. Fortunately they have not needed to follow her other, sadder path in which Diana learned that her own unhappiness created a powerful affinity with some of the world's most excluded and stigmatized people.

Diana's experience of separation and divorce has perhaps surprising resonance for Meghan in explaining some of the pressures and challenges of royal marriage management. Getting the balance right between public duty and private happiness might turn out to be her greatest achievement.

Meanwhile, other crucial balances must be struck, such as: tradition versus innovation, regal restraint versus passionate campaigning, privacy versus publicity, and spontaneity versus dogged persistence. It's a long list, and in tackling it Meghan will depend crucially on empathy with the ordinary citizens of her adopted country and on her own internal judgement. As she may already have guessed, as a real royal highness she'll have access to an infinite supply of advice, but in the end, only *she* can decide how to take control of the extraordinary destiny providence has placed in her hands.

Then there are the in-laws. A royal newcomer could ask for no better role model than Elizabeth II, whose lifetime of dedicated public service sets a standard unlikely to be bettered in the whole history of the British Crown. Eventually, and many pray it will be far off, Elizabeth's place on the throne will be taken by Meghan's father-in-law, Prince Charles. He and his controversial second wife, Camilla, offer her a mixed buffet of how-to-be-royal experience. And of course, when she needs counsel from somebody her own age, William and Catherine will be her neighbors in Kensington Palace.

Not the least of Meghan's challenges will be the speed with which she'll have to assimilate the constitutional instincts that her new position in the British hierarchy will demand. Being American is an attractive novelty—for now. How she retains the best of her native heritage and combines it with the distinctive qualities of Britishness will be a process under constant review. Against a backdrop of transatlantic cultural complexity, this may sometimes make the ocean feel very wide.

The best news for her, for Harry, and for an expectant British public is that if she gets it right, the reward will be the secure evolution of the great institution that has welcomed her—and two lives made complete by their service to humanity.

# CHAPTER 1

# In the Shadow of Diana

*"I don't go by the rule book; I lead from the heart, not the head."*
*—Princess Diana*

Midwinter in Manhattan. From the Carlyle Hotel on the Upper East Side to the Hilton ballroom on Sixth Avenue has taken the royal limousine, with its impressive NYPD and Secret Service convoy of escorting vehicles, less than fifteen minutes through the evening rush-hour traffic. Waiting on the sidewalk is a crowd of several hundred enthusiastic onlookers, waving from behind police crowd barriers, their smiling faces stark in the television lights. The welcoming committee, led by Dr. Henry Kissinger, takes its assigned places and prepares its royal small talk.

Clustered in the press pen, the familiar A-team of media photographers prepares to go to work, aiming their Nikons at the door of the limousine, ready for their favorite royal subject to reveal herself and—just as important—her choice of evening gown for what is being trumpeted as New York's most prestigious social gathering of the year.

A Secret Service agent takes one last look up and down the street and opens the limousine door. The crowd presses forward as the cheers rise to a crescendo. With practiced elegance America's favorite princess steps onto the red carpet, a figure at once familiar and fabulously fresh, radiating a glamour that any film star would recognize as Hollywood plus. As her entourage hangs back to give the fans and the cameras an uninterrupted view, the Princess rewards Dr. Kissinger's warm embrace with a double kiss and then allows herself to be escorted into the hotel and out of sight. As for her gown, it's hidden under a long dark coat against the evening chill but later reveals itself to be a plunging, dark blue, sequined number.

The entourage hurries to keep up while on the sidewalk the happy crowd excitedly shares their impressions of their brief glimpse of real British royalty. The photographers climb down from their stepladders and prepare to move to the next photo opportunity. The rush-hour traffic resumes its usual high tempo, heedless of the star-spotting opportunity it has just missed.

Princess Di is back in New York, a city she loved—and which loved her. Royalty and America: it's a thrilling mix…

I was a member of the tuxedo-clad posse that surged after Princess Diana into the lofty hotel foyer, where crowds of happily surprised hotel guests were taking the opportunity to enjoy a close-up view of this unexpected extra entertainment. Actually, I was somewhere near the head of the entourage having driven with the Princess in the limousine. As happened so often, I was trying to keep out of the way of the security agents while staying close enough to the Princess so she could turn and slip me a few *sotto voce* words without having to break stride. This sometimes took quite a bit of fancy footwork, but luckily I had had plenty of practice. As her private secretary/chief of staff I had been directing this rather exclusive roadshow for nearly eight years, accompanying it to every corner of the world from these familiar streets of New York to the wilds of the Himalayas, the hubbub of Hong Kong, the boulevards of Paris, and many more.

When not on the road I spent my days either in the office at St. James's Palace or at Princess Diana's apartment in Kensington Palace. During those years, wherever I found myself I had never been able to escape, or in truth, had never wished to escape, from the relentless drama that accompanied the acrimonious collapse of Diana's marriage to Prince Charles, or the giddy rocket-powered trajectory of her seemingly unstoppable rise in worldwide fame and popularity.

Those years had seen Princess Diana emerge from her husband's shadow to become an icon of glamour and compassion, embracing controversial humanitarian causes such as AIDS, leprosy, addiction, and mental illness in a way that revolutionized perceptions of how royalty and charities could work together. It was no coincidence that she devoted herself year after year to causes that focused on the plight of the excluded and stigmatized because, as she told me, "I understand them, Patrick, because I'm one of them."

And so she was, not through poverty or physical suffering, but through her unhappy journey from future queen, on the arm of a protective husband in 1981, to royal outcast in 1995. It was as an outcast that she attended that New York event, which in its stripped-down protocol subtly hinted at her lack of a defined royal role. Nevertheless, through its obvious glamor and media power, it also sent a message to those back home who wanted to clip her wings: this divorcing princess has reserves of determination and global influence that may surprise you.

I had joined Diana's organization as an equerry (military aide) in 1988, becoming her full-time private secretary in 1990, just in time to begin the task of creating a new royal household for Diana, who already saw her separation from Prince Charles on the horizon.

As I labored to set up and run the kind of modest but hard-working support team that suited her unique royal style—a demanding mix of utter perfection and split-second spontaneity—it was no surprise that I and all those others who supported Diana's rollercoaster royal progress felt ourselves privileged to be part of a challenging but inspiring experiment in how our part of the House of Windsor might adapt that ancient dynasty to a world that wanted more than a distant wave and stilted platitudes. If what we were doing unsettled some of the more traditional elements from less friendly corners of the royal universe—not the least from her estranged husband's circle of friends and advisers—that was fine with us, especially since nobody could ever find the smallest fault with the professionalism and dedication that were the hallmarks of how Diana did her duty for the Crown.

Nevertheless, although tonight's engagement was in many ways routine, and organizationally very much at the easier end the scale, for me it was anything but normal. This was because, still unknown to the Princess, I had already decided to resign from her service. For all the well-practiced efficiency of tonight's event at the Hilton, the rest of Diana's life and, in particular, its next few steps, were becoming a confusing jumble in which her future status and occupation seemed as unclear as her own intentions.

Since giving a self-sabotaging interview to the BBC peak-time current affairs program *Panorama* just a couple of weeks previously, it had seemed that her life and mine were in a kind of freefall—where we would land and what we would do when we got there were fast becoming questions I no longer wished to try to answer. Contributing to my reluctant decision was Diana's increasing tendency to seek advice from those who saw her as a useful vehicle for their own agendas, and to portray herself as a victim of events rather than as the strong and influential woman I knew her to be, well able to decide her own destiny.

Perhaps crucially in my thinking, the Princess, for reasons that I understood given her mixed feelings of abandonment and defiance, had chosen to chop away the time-tested structure of royal status and support that had protected her in a dangerous world, even as she chafed against its constraints.

I was part of that structure, happy to be so even as I had set aside my obligations to my own young family. The demands of being "the producer of the Diana show" as the Oscar-winning head of Columbia Studios David Puttnam had described me, demanded every ounce of commitment and probably more. Combined, all these separate straws were putting the camel's back of my loyalty under a strain I no longer felt able to tolerate. So her starring role at tonight's glittering New York awards ceremony was to be the last event for which I would accompany my boss onto the supersonic Concorde airliner across the Atlantic.

The watching guests took hurried photographs of our preening black-tied gaggle, with the Princess the dazzling gem at its center, as it surged across the lobby and up the stairs to the ballroom. Already most of the expected 1,500 guests were at their tables, filling the enormous space with a cheerful cacophony of excited conversation and the expensive potpourri of scores of competing perfumes. The guest list was drawn from the highest strata of New York society as well as including Secretary of State Henry Kissinger and General (later Secretary of State) Colin Powell, accompanied by media mogul Rupert Murdoch, who hosted the royal guest alongside the head of the charity honoring her, United Cerebral Palsy of New York.

This was definitely the place to be, not just because of Princess Diana's presence but also to witness her acceptance of the Humanitarian of the Year award. This was an honor she had tried to resist, not the least of which on the grounds that her job as a princess meant that she should be giving awards, not receiving them. But the organizers had been politely insistent and, given the fundraising potential of such an evening for their good cause, the Princess had agreed, with just the right degree of gracious reluctance.

The evening was a total success. When it came to staging top-level events on this scale the Hilton certainly knew how to impress. The wine, the dinner, the accompanying live music, all contributed to the sense of celebration and when her hosts rose to praise the Princess and catalogue her impressive contributions to humanitarian causes during her royal career thus far, the room was united in its admiration of the smiling but attractively diffident award recipient. As usual, she hit all the right notes as she teased General Powell about his claim that they were distant kinsmen, expressed her support for the charity, and acknowledged her gratitude for the honor it was bestowing on her.

Except, perhaps the room was not quite united, as a lone voice interrupted her speech with a question:

"Where are your kids, Di?"

There was a universal offended intake of breath but without missing a beat, Diana turned in the direction of the voice and assured everyone that her children were at school. Given the time difference, and the fact that they were at boarding school, this meant that they were safely in bed. Having thus rebutted the implied criticism that she was a neglectful mother, she returned unruffled to her text. The applause was loud, heartfelt, and prolonged.

Much later, when her distinguished hosts had seen her to the curbside, and the fans who had waited in the cold for her to reappear had been treated to personal words of thanks, the royal visitor got back into her limousine, waving a final fond farewell as she drove away.

Sitting beside her in the dark I watched the flashing lights of the escort as we were shepherded along the still busy streets back to the sanctuary of the hotel on East 76th Street. The Carlyle had, by this time, become Diana's New York home away from home, and she was in relaxed mood when we stepped out of the elevator and were escorted to her penthouse suite. As sometimes happened after a particularly good day she invited me in for a glass of champagne (Louis Roederer Cristal, if I remember correctly) and a jolly good gossip about the people and events that were her most entertaining memories of the last few hours.

These were the kind of moments that had been a reward for me for years that I was happy to accept, in return for a life totally dedicated to a royal cause that I believed deserved everything I could give it.

I had been carrying the humanitarian award—a bold modern design in granite and glass—ever since we had left the Hilton and now I carefully placed it on a side table. Turning to the Princess and raising my glass I said:

"All these years I've been flying around the world telling people you didn't accept awards—your job was to hand them out. But I think you were right to accept this one. You've certainly earned it."

She briefly raised her eyebrows, then turned to look out at the nighttime Manhattan skyline. With her eyes still fixed on the famous panorama she thought for a moment, then replied, "No, Patrick, I don't deserve this." She looked at me and raised her glass in turn. "But I am *working* on it!"

That phrase summed up her vision of herself, and her future, however uncertain it might be. Not a bad poster image for a very successful brand of royalty: modesty and determination, with a glass of champagne, while still looking like the proverbial million dollars. It was an especially effective visual message when seen alongside that other classic image of Princess Diana: in chinos and open neck shirt while holding a sick African baby.

Of course, it's the modesty and determination that earned her something far more valuable than just success—it was recognized and rewarded with an enduring affection from stigmatized and excluded people all over the world.

More than twenty years after that New York awards dinner, those same qualities have been recognized in Diana's children who, no longer asleep in their spartan school dorms, have grown into their own distinctive style of royal humanitarian work. But for anyone interested in the origins of their present and future charitable ambitions—a wife, for example—that New York night and their mother's down-to-earth assessment of her own value and potential might make a relevant case study.

Twenty years after his mother's death, one of those sons, whose bedtime was momentarily so important at that Hilton dinner, has chosen a bride. In a coincidental but happy piece of symmetry, he has chosen an American, Meghan Markle. And in a further subliminal connection, Ms. Markle is the same age now that Prince Harry's mother had just reached at the time of her tragically early death in a Paris car crash. An alignment of the stars that surely augurs well for the couple.

The stars have already been kind to Harry's elder brother, the future King William, currently Duke of Cambridge. He and Duchess Catherine, together with their attractively unstuffy young family, have earned their positions as the popular and wholesome long-term face of the British monarchy, an institution that has had more than its fair share of less-than-wholesome headlines in the past few decades.

Many of those miserable media memories concerned the international disappointment, at times verging on despair, caused by the marital woes of William and Harry's parents, Prince Charles and Princess Diana. Their acrimonious, well-publicized, and divisive divorce cast a long shadow over royal life, not helped by Prince Charles's controversial remarriage to the divorced Mrs. Camilla Parker-Bowles, his long-term mistress and a central figure in his divorce from Diana.

Now at last, not least thanks to British nationwide rejoicing over William and Catherine's marriage in 2010, that shadow has been largely lifted. Both princes now speak openly about their mother in a way that carries the true resonance of their freely expressed love of the woman whose memory and achievements they celebrate, even as they still openly (and bravely) grieve for all that they have lost.

From the earliest days of royal legend, princesses have been attributed mesmerizing qualities of beauty, grace, insight, and often, tragedy. Diana was just the latest in the line of princesses stretching back to the earliest days of the British monarchy, a famously gutsy and glamorous tribe to which she brought a whole new style of girl-next-door accessibility that she could switch, in classic royal style, into an icy aristocratic remoteness in the blink of an eye.

Now this intimidating bloodline of pedigreed royal females is about to admit its newest member. Like it or not, Ms. Meghan Markle will be judged by standards that have never been successfully defined and that cannot be found in any reference book or on any website, yet a watching world—and history—will ruthlessly apply them to Meghan when deciding her success or failure as a princess.

Add to this intimidating prospect the familiar challenges facing every bride and mother-in-law relationship and Meghan might be said to have her work cut out for her. The fact that in this case the mother-in-law is

Princess Diana, who has already passed into a realm of untouchable and ageless perfection, may make this relationship a little more complicated.

As always, though, the shade of Diana can be both an intimidating presence and a guiding inspiration. While no wise princess (or duchess for that matter) would presume to trespass on Diana's place in the world's affections, let alone on her sons' memories, for Meghan the opportunity now beckons to study Diana both as an example and as a warning, and to draw on those two treasure houses of experience while taking control of her own royal destiny.

Of all the things she is learning about becoming a princess, none will be more important for Meghan than what she is told—or is able to discover—about the woman who, were she still alive, would be her guide, philosopher, mentor, friend and, almost inevitably, sometimes her kindest critic, keenest competitor, and sense-of-humor tester as well.

Meghan will already have noticed that Diana occupies a strange place in Windsor family history. The next king's dead ex-wife who, in the eyes of many, tainted the royal brand with scandal and emotional incontinence, is bound to be a difficult subject to discuss in polite royal circles.

Diana's other persona, as hard-working single mother, channeling her own unhappiness to the benefit of some of the world's least popular and neglected humanitarian issues, may be the one most familiar to the Californian divorced actress who has built her own international reputation for supporting difficult causes.

Add a layer of Diana's topical feminist grit and you have a role model that any aspiring princess might be grateful to study. And that's in addition to what are surely the most heartfelt and moving tributes to his mother she will surely always hear from her husband.

However, what Meghan may not hear elsewhere is that Diana was a reluctant rebel. Had the necessary courtesy, respect, encouragement, and patience (especially patience) been found to guide her undoubted but volatile gifts, the tragedy of her separation from Prince Charles could most likely have been avoided. So too, the loss to the Royal Family of her charisma, work ethic, and uncanny ability to read the public mood.

In happy contrast, the William and Kate story-so-far suggests that today's royal brides can expect the path of royal love to be a little less rocky. Unlike the nineteen-year-old Diana, Meghan holds many of the keys to her destiny in her own hands and will surely be blessed with a husband who gives her needs, ambitions, and happiness at least equal priority to his own.

Ultimately, it will be where Meghan turns for advice that will determine much of her success or failure as a princess. It is a blessing, and a curse, that royal people can choose from a limitless smorgasbord of advice: good, bad, and indifferent. Making the right choices is perhaps the single most important factor in royal survival, popularity, and peace of mind.

Members of the British Royal Family still wield extraordinary, and largely unaccountable, influence and prestige. In the end, Meghan is likely to discover that the only form of discipline to guide her use of these new super powers will be the kind she imposes on herself. That's where we, and her new in-laws, may gratefully find that a life already marked by tough decisions and hard experience is Meghan's best possible preparation for the unprecedented privilege she will enjoy.

# CHAPTER 2

# Meghan—Your Endless Audition Starts Here

*"There is no better time to really continue to shine a light upon women feeling empowered."*
*—Ms. Meghan Markle*

Much has been written, and more will no doubt continue to emerge, about the pre-royal life of Meghan Markle. In sharp contrast with most new princesses, she arrives on the royal stage as a fully formed person in her own right—and an actress to boot. At thirty-six she has already equaled the lifespan of Harry's mother, a mathematically neat coincidence, albeit with slightly unsettling psychological undertones. Comparisons to Diana may lift Meghan with inspiration or nccdlc hcr with frustration—probably both at times—but it's likely they will be her lifelong companions.

The examples and warnings of the Diana story could usefully be the never-ending homework of any Windsor recruit, the more so for being largely avoided and thus probably misunderstood subjects in polite royal society. If you're an apprentice at the trade of regal smiles and waves, one above all others should be your priority: the distinction between celebrity and royalty. The line between the two has always been vague. If you can't go to your local supermarket on Kensington High Street without causing a minor riot or ride the London tube without a security detail, your high recognition factor could easily confuse people (you most of all) into thinking your very existence is cause for celebration. For someone who has devoted so much of her energy to acquiring that very celebrity status, the task of distinguishing between fame you've earned and fame you've acquired through accident of birth or marriage must be harder still.

If you haven't worked out the difference yet—and hopefully you did so before slipping on the engagement ring—now is the time to get it clear in your own mind and in everybody else's. Get it wrong, as your well-intentioned but ill-advised uncle-in-law Edward notoriously did with his catastrophic attempt to mix royalty and showbiz (if you haven't already done so, be sure to Google *"It's a Royal Knockout")* and you may never be entirely forgiven. This is even more relevant since, sadly, there will always be skeptics ready to wonder if your new life as a royal highness is really an unconditional surrender to the call of true love or just the most successful offensive yet in a long-running fame campaign.

The key is to remember that although many of the perks and outward trappings of royalty and celebrity are identical, the defining difference is that celebrity lifestyles are won, while royal privileges are granted. Both can be taken away by the fickle court of public opinion, while royal privileges are always at the mercy of royal displeasure.

In the royal world, as with so much else, a different code of cause and effect prevails. Some familiarity with the fates of Kings Charles I, James II, and Edward VIII (and, perhaps, the wives of Henry VIII) would be useful here. The withdrawal of privileges is likely to take longer than it does to axe a dud television series, and the consequences—such as beheading, takeover by a foreign royal housc, or national constitutional crisis—are really much, much harder to live with.

The apparent permanence of Meghan's new surroundings and the current high approval ratings of the organization she is joining should not lull her into forgetting that these blessings will only be reliably delivered in return for a life devoted to the service of the subjects of the Crown, preferably with lots of visible, unenviable duty and the unmistakable appearance of sacrifice. Otherwise, all the clever publicists in the world—and all the reassuring sycophancy of her court—won't save her from disaster.

If looking for an example of an early sacrifice she might usefully make, Meghan could take an early vow to deny herself all activity or communication that might be interpreted as a comment on politics or public policy. Her father-in-law has enjoyed stirring up controversy on a wide range of semi-political topics—to the delight or dismay of his future ministers and subjects, according to partisan political taste—but her reputation won't survive theatrical interventions in areas that rightly belong to private citizens or elected politicians.

Of course, in an option also open to Prince Charles, once she has her new British passport, and has probably renounced her American one, she could run for office and let the ballot box give her the right to intervene on any subject that troubled her constituents. But otherwise she must keep her personal opinions strictly private. In this context, her widely advertised pre-Harry support for Democratic politics in her home country is a piece of personal baggage that must now be jettisoned: the sacred royal duty of political neutrality doesn't end at the shores of the kingdom. This is doubly true now that she is becoming part of the British ruling establishment and will therefore inevitably sometimes be seen to be acting as some form of conduit for official UK thinking (this risk is especially acute in countries unblessed by centuries of democratic evolution).

Of course, that doesn't mean that she can't take a stand on humanitarian issues. In fact, she has giddy powers of choice to decide which are worthy of the prestige and big donors' largesse that she can deliver in huge quantities. Princess Diana was fabulously effective at communicating a strong humanitarian message just with a well-arranged photograph, and Meghan will doubtless develop these and other techniques to leverage her suddenly global power to influence. Meanwhile, her good causes will be particularly grateful when she perfects the delicate art of loosening the purse strings of potential benefactors, many of whom secretly enjoy nothing more than a pretty princessly shakedown, preferably on the dance floor at a glamorous charity ball.

Even then, this is a power to be exercised with judicious caution. If in doubt, she and her advisors should remember one of *Downton Abbey*'s best lines: "The truth is neither here nor there. It's the look of the thing that matters."

This warning is especially relevant when enjoying a run of particularly favorable headlines and generally surfing on waves of royal good fortune. The Romans had a very effective way of reminding even triumphant conquerors of their mortality: they positioned a slave to stand behind the victor and repeat in his ear that he was not a god, but still only a man, even as he enjoyed a glorious chariot lap of honor past crowds of cheering plebs.

The modern royal equivalent of that chariot ride is a rain-soaked line of citizens, shivering under a winter sky against a grey backdrop of industrial inner-city decline.

They've been standing there for hours, penned by steel crowd barriers under the watchful eye of damp and unamused police officers, waiting for just one thing: the chance to see you up close, maybe call a warm greeting and offer a drooping little posy of flowers, maybe even shake your hand and get a gracious, friendly word in return.

These are your people—and you are their princess. This is royal duty and public devotion of intoxicating purity. And it's for *you*. Look again at the people. See the world through their eyes, and your place in it.

Now…where is the slave with the warning in your ear? If you listen carefully, he isn't whispering "tell them about #MeToo" or "don't forget #TimesUp."

Nobody can doubt Meghan's sincerity when she says, "Right now with so many campaigns like #MeToo and #TimesUp there's no better time to continue to shine a light on women feeling empowered and people supporting them."

However, a glance at her new country will remind her that the perspective that draws such warm applause in California awards ceremonies may need adjusting in a nation currently led by its second female prime minister, and which has had the benefit of a female head of state for more than sixty years.

On further reflection, her advisers may also feel uneasy about an attitude that so readily excludes half the population, a half that, for all its faults, needs to feel that its problems are no less sincerely appreciated by the Royal Family. They may go on to hope that not too many people will recall that quite a few members of the Royal Family are men, and that not all of them have always achieved #MeToo-approved standards of correct male behavior.

So even on subjects about which she feels passionately, Meghan can afford to modulate her delivery. Being royal means that you will automatically always be heard, even when you whisper. It's a magic power, given to very few and earned by even fewer. Unlike a struggling actress, a royal princess will be listened to, respectfully and in silence, bar a few polite laughs at the right points. There will be reliable applause afterwards, no matter how half-baked or obvious the royal remarks might have been. This readily given approval can all too easily give the speaker an inflated and dangerously misleading perception of their own oratory and intellect. There are plenty of examples of this phenomenon which Meghan's advisers can draw to her attention.

They might remind her too that the British Royal Family usually does best when it follows the example of the present queen who, as constitutional monarchs must, acts only on the advice of her ministers. Taking the trouble to find out current government policy, identify the bits that align with your own agenda, and tailor any public remarks accordingly requires quite a lot of preparation and research, and may feel a bit restrictive. However, it's a necessary chore if she wants to show that she understands her place in the largely un-signposted constitutional landscape of which she is now a very visible feature.

The success of William, Kate, and Harry's "Heads Together" campaign to raise awareness of mental health issues owes much to its careful coordination with the UK's Department of Health and Social Care. Such coordination with the legislative and executive branches of government is always time well spent and can protect the earnest royal campaigner from publicly contradicting a new flagship policy announced hours earlier by a cabinet minister. The voters understand that—at least theoretically—their elected representatives will answer at the next election if they don't deliver the services they've promised. The voters also understand (as the media will quickly remind them) that royal people are not elected, and any inclination to listen to their views on any subject is an act of courtesy.

Luckily the British people tend to be very courteous, especially to royal highnesses, and cut them slack a politician can only envy. And though Meghan's father-in-law, Prince Charles, has long enjoyed sharing (some might say oversharing) with steadfastly polite audiences whatever is currently vexing him, this is not an envelope a wise royal campaigner should push. A newcomer even less so. A proven ability to listen and learn, and look attractively thoughtful while doing so, is an essential precursor to any plans for humanitarian global domination that may be brewing in a royal brain.

It follows that any ambition Meghan may have to use her new royal platform as a launchpad for worldwide humanitarian initiatives must be tempered with a clear understanding of how that platform was built, who pays for it, and how readily it can be dismantled. Nothing will get the dismantling crews busy quicker than royal sermons on politically contentious issues.

If Meghan has studied the experience of those who have trodden an earlier path into the heart of planet Windsor, she will have noticed that the ones who prosper are those who have successfully proved their ability to practice a vital skill. Contrary to what some ill-informed observers may think, the essential qualification isn't an encyclopedic knowledge of obscure palace protocol or knowing how and when to curtsey (and to whom). Nor is it the ability to maintain a diplomatically acceptable level of small talk with a halitosis-stricken visiting head of state. Nor even is it a talent for getting out of a low-slung limousine in a low-cut evening gown while maintaining the highest standards of modesty. Least of all is it a gift for attracting huge crowds of adoring new fans (or acres of drooling newsprint): any aptitude Meghan may exhibit for inspiring this kind of result—and she has already shown plenty—will not necessarily endear her to every fellow member of the royal cast.

All of these count as useful capabilities, but they are all essentially secondary. Instead, the one really key skill Meghan absolutely must perfect is how to avoid being seen as any kind of a destabilizing danger to the established royal order. In the whispering labyrinth of the court, unexpected surprises, even nice ones, can be misinterpreted as threats. Anything new or unknown, until it is proven to be harmless, will therefore be treated with suspicion, even hostility. Centuries of royal history have shown that, when you're in the dynasty business, every consideration is subjected to the ultimate existential test: will this person/thing/idea/development help or hinder the survival of the current royal line?

Especially in the early days—no, make that years—Meghan needs to work on getting a resounding *Yes*, every time this unspoken question is asked about her.

Nobody who walks on palace red carpet would admit as much, but it's a useful guideline when weighing the pros and cons of any intended course of action, from saving a local preschool play group, to saving an endangered species, to saving the very future of the planet: what always comes first is saving the monarchy (something the first line of the British national anthem conveniently reminds us).

Because the Crown is an ancient institution, its time horizons are set to infinity, at least compared to most other aspects of modern life. Unlike a political party, it doesn't depend on anything as dreary as ballot box success for its survival. Nor is it a mighty corporation that must maintain an inexorable rise in stock price to retain its market mojo. Least of all does it resemble a Hollywood production, chained to the tyranny of viewing figures or in thrall to investors and critics.

Yet for all its apparent permanence and stately, glacial rate of evolution, it depends for its survival on a very volatile commodity: the benign approval, or at the very least willing tolerance, of its subjects. And these days, don't forget these are the ordinary people who pay the taxes that fund the grants that settle the bills that keep the essential parts of the royal machine moving smoothly.

Significantly, when the option of replacing the monarch with an elected head of state has been put to the test (Australia being a good example) voters have backed retaining the existing unelected regal figurehead. And while some have interpreted this as good news for long-term royal survival, others have pointed out that such results may owe more to the personal popularity of Elizabeth II and the unappetizing nature of most of the likely political/presidential alternatives than to any undying love of the Windsors.

As Diana discovered to her cost, if you acquire for yourself, however justifiably, a profile, a purpose, and a vocal, passionate public devotion independent of the royal mainstream, then you will risk being perceived and presented as a threat to the Crown itself. This will mobilize the full forces of the establishment against you, and in defense of itself, it won't feel constrained by any fluffy notions of good old-fashioned British gentlemanly fair play.

If deep-rooted royal insecurity is one threat to be managed, there's another that requires no less vigilance. While public love of the Crown may be a complex blend of emotion and self-interest, love of individual members of the Royal Family is usually pretty unambiguous, and only to be confronted at your peril. Of course, like all human love, it can be withdrawn (sometimes at very short notice) but in the case of Princes William and Harry—especially Harry—it is an authentically powerful force. What's more, it's virtually impossible to control and is remarkably resistant to any counteracting arguments. Just look at the emotions roused by the twentieth anniversary of Princess Diana's death, despite a determined campaign to marginalize and downgrade her contribution to public life.

Memories of the last American divorcee to marry into the Royal Family are long, unhappy, and regularly refreshed. As a result, despite predictable and welcome displays of public warmth towards Ms. Markle, she begins her duties under an unspoken form of probation. There is no lack of desire to see she and her husband installed as happy and glorious additions to the pantheon of successful and beloved royal couples. But most of that warmth is directed at Harry and would be shared by pretty much anyone he chose to marry.

What's more, it's a warmth that owes nothing to constitutional pragmatism since, given the happy viability of the Cambridge mini dynasty, neither Harry nor Meghan will ever ascend the throne. So, even more than most royal newcomers, Meghan will be judged by her success as the never-failing source to her husband of strength, comfort, encouragement, and wisdom. If she falls short in these areas, allows any doubt in suspicious minds that she is anything less than devoted to her man, his family, and her obligations to her adopted country... then she may not have the luxury of any second chances.

In those circumstances, Meghan, or anybody on her behalf, should think long and carefully before reaching for the race card as a response to unfavorable news stories. The new princess's diverse ancestry is a positive asset for the House of Windsor, as its members and supporters are well aware. Beyond that, all the powers of anti-hate crime legislation are available to them, given sufficient grounds. It would be tragic if Meghan or her husband got into the habit of firing ethnic warning shots at a media which, like it or not, will be their lifelong companions, especially when the same media will reliably trumpet all their good work…so long as there's lots of it.

# CHAPTER 3

# Golden Twilight—Elizabeth's Long Autumn

*"I have in sincerity pledged myself to your service, as so many of you are pledged to mine. Throughout all my life and with all my heart I shall strive to be worthy of your trust."*
*—HM The Queen*

It seems very likely that future historians will look back at the closing years of Elizabeth II's reign as the slow, stately demise of a golden age. Television series like

*The Crown,* for all their gleefully detected historical inaccuracies, have helped new generations feel a sense of what it must have been like to have such a beautiful and vulnerable, yet also strong and dutiful young queen on the throne.

When Elizabeth married in November 1947, aged just twenty-one, she and her handsome Royal Navy Lieutenant fiancé epitomized a generation that sacrificed its youth to the fight against the evils of totalitarianism. She had also served in uniform, trained how to service and maintain army vehicles and could legitimately share a measure of the suffering caused by the Luftwaffe's bombing campaign, during which her own home of Buckingham Palace had been severely damaged. Wartime shortages still lingered, and she famously had to use clothing ration coupons to buy her dress.

As the visible, tangible link to the mythology of "the Greatest Generation," Elizabeth has been a remote-yet-beloved mother and grandmother figure to baby boomers and their children. A world without her is as hard to imagine as the London skyline without Tower Bridge. Yet like Tower Bridge, Elizabeth's reign may come to be seen be seen as a product of the Victorian age, its original imperial inspirational power giving way to an uncertain vision of its future purpose in which nostalgia and hope mix uneasily with celebrity and entitlement.

Comparing Elizabeth with Victoria will probably become an increasingly popular pastime for royal commentators. But one resemblance that is often overlooked is the degree to which the two queens bookend a century where, time and again, it has been the women of the family who have kept the royal ship afloat, from stoic Alexandra, who endured the serial infidelities of Edward VII, to unbending Mary of Teck, who gave spine and humanity to the reign of George V, to gutsy Queen Elizabeth the Queen Mother.

The universally popular "Queen Mum" gave both stuttering George VI and a beleaguered Britain a figurehead of doughty patriotism who, with her crowd-pleasing public appearances, simultaneously earned the Windsors some well-timed classless credentials. She thus added valuable extra capital to the bank of royal goodwill during bleak years of wartime struggle and postwar austerity, just when several of Europe's lesser monarchies were being driven into oblivion. Her daughter's sense of duty, typified by this chapter's opening quotation, reinforces the image of a gallery of powerful royal women, keeping watch over their successors and reminding them by their example what it means to wear royal status with ease and also, crucially, to understand its nature and purpose.

The present Queen's life of service has already surpassed all others in longevity and can claim similar ascendancy in selfless duty and sacrifice. A line from a public promise she made on her twenty-first birthday is worth quoting in full:

> *"I declare before you all that my whole life whether it be long or short shall be devoted to your service."*

Those words, and the age at which they were spoken, may be as far as any royal highness need look for inspiration, or for a clearer understanding that royal status must be continually re-earned through sacrifice.

The concept of sacrifice as compensation for royal privilege has been embodied by these women in a way that their husbands and sons struggled to achieve. Only perhaps in William and Harry will the pattern be reversed, provided the principle of self-denial in return for lives of right royal privilege is regularly observed—by them and their wives and children. Neglect it, and the benign public indifference that is the Windsors' most undervalued, underrecognized, but undoubtedly most precious asset, could evaporate with bewildering speed.

Here once again, William and Harry's mother may serve as a relatable example to these and future royal wives. As a doomed personification of duty, hope, and tragedy, it is hardly a stretch to see in Diana, the teen-aged royal *ingénue,* a sacrifice to the cause of dynastic continuation and renewal.

The Crown may have been a heavy burden for Elizabeth, but at least she has never given any public sign that she doubted either its relevance or its purpose. As clear as her understanding of what it was *for* has been her instinct for what it was *not for.* Such instincts are vital in the British constitutional system, which, being largely unwritten, depends on shared interpretation of tradition and precedent.

It took hundreds of years for the will of the people to challenge, trim, and finally extinguish the executive powers of the monarch—from King John and the Magna Carta right up to vestigial regal prerogatives in present times. What is left was described by Winston Churchill (a devoted monarchist, who defended Edward VIII's wish to marry a woman deemed unacceptable by Church and government) as a crowned republic....

> *"In our island, by trial and error, and by perseverance across the centuries we have found a very good plan. Here it is: The Queen can do no wrong, but advisers can be changed as often as the people like to use their right for that purpose."*

Somewhere even in today's Windsor DNA is the memory of what the people will do if sufficiently provoked, the public execution of their ancestor King Charles I being just the most vivid of many examples.

Despite having potentially the most powerful platform on which to share her views, insights, big ideas, wishes, and prejudices, Elizabeth has resolutely kept her opinions, especially on the politics of the day, strictly to herself. The wisdom of her self-imposed silence becomes all the deeper when you consider that, though shorn of executive power, the British Royal Family retains enormous potential to influence public mood and opinion and, even, government action.

Harry's father, Prince Charles, fully recognizes the potential of this power of influence. But unlike his instinctively circumspect mother, he uses it regularly to air his own views and the agendas of people and organizations whose views he wishes to promote. This "convening" of groups who might otherwise miss opportunities for joint action, or for fundraising, is an astute use of royal patronage and assets such as palace banqueting facilities. Through unabashed use of his status as the next head of state and a sophisticated in-house staff of policy specialists and media experts, he has, in many respects, assumed the role of a shadow but unaccountable arm of government.

The Prince's advocacy of causes is defended by some as a means to maintain the relevance of the office he will inherit; others, more skeptical, may see that as a thin disguise for constitutionally risky mission-creep. Either way, having stepped onto the sensitive territory of public policy debate, Prince Charles seems to welcome any controversy that results, once referring to himself approvingly as "a subversive." Unsurprisingly, perhaps, for a future king, no such approval is likely for subversives in his own organization. A more disturbing aspect of this para-political activity has been his advisors' embrace of political-style communications techniques, misapplying the dark arts of spin to the delicate task of securing the dynasty. This mix of intervention, subversion, and media manipulation is one the next generation would surely be wise not to emulate.

A systematic campaign to diminish the character and achievements of his ex-wife in favor of his mistress, Camilla Parker Bowles, is but one example of the distinctly ungracious activities of this palace misinformation squad. A simultaneous investment in digital marketing and social media has ensured a historically unparalleled size of audience for royal opinions. The reach and effectiveness of this output is supercharged by state-of-the-art digital marketing techniques, which sit uneasily in an institution that owes its survival to public affection for historical continuity.

These recent advances in royal communications power can't now be uninvented, but they should attract a correspondingly raised awareness among royal people and their advisors that such wonder-weapons could easily backfire spectacularly.

The British take justified pride in the scarcity of revolutions in their history. With rare exceptions, change has come slowly and peacefully through an evolutionary democratic progress. Paroxysms of internal conflict have been seen as the fate of foreign—and, by implication, inferior—countries. Generations of English kings and queens defined their foreign policy by their enmity for rival European rulers, especially the kings of France. So we might bet that eighteenth-century English royalty and its supporters among the noble classes felt more than a little anxious about the French Revolution of 1789, which saw not just the French king and his family lose their heads, but also much of the aristocratic class whose loyalty had given him legitimacy.

Even in what for the Windsors is recent family history, it was not them but their foreign cousins who ignominiously lost their thrones: Czar Nicholas of Russia and Kaiser Wilhelm of Germany are just two examples but right across Europe, from Italy, Greece, and Albania to Austria, Spain, and Portugal the twentieth century saw the demise of royal houses that had reigned collectively for thousands of years with every appearance of indestructibility.[1]

There is no universal law that says the British Crown will forever escape the fates of its European neighbors and relations. Although King Farooq of Egypt may have joked that along with the kings of Diamonds, Clubs,

---

1 Notably, however, Spain restored its monarchy after the Franco dictatorship (1939-75).

Hearts, and Spades the only surviving royal family would eventually be England's, other less friendly views may one day prevail.

Postponing that day is the unwritten first duty of those in the British royal dynasty business. Thus recent decades have seen previously unimaginable shifts towards a more modern style of monarchy such as the payment of income tax, opening the royal palaces to suitably ticketed visitors, a more liberal attitude to divorce and, most recently, a readiness to marry not just commoners but even, whisper it, foreign, divorced commoners of ethnically diverse ancestry.

The success of recent moves to popularize the anachronism of royalty in the twenty-first century, and the undoubted media appeal of its younger members, have distracted from the reality that the entire institution depends for its survival on the support—or at least the acquiescence—of the populations of the United Kingdom and the sixteen Commonwealth Realms (such as Canada, Australia, and New Zealand) and the fourteen British Overseas Territories, such as Bermuda, Gibraltar, the Cayman Islands, and the Falklands.

William and Harry's modern ancestors recognized that their position at the head of society depended on public perception that their privileges were earned through duty and sacrifice. There is now a new risk, through the blurring of the line separating royalty from celebrity, that this time-honored convention will be forgotten, coming to mind only in a crisis and then quite possibly too late.

It was Louis XIV of France who presciently said, "*Après moi le déluge.*" In just two generations his grandiose and apparently invincible royal house was a ruin, spattered with the blood of his descendants. The guillotine may never be erected in Trafalgar Square, but a fickle public mood multiplied by merciless digital media has the capacity to decapitate an unpopular royal family—or family member—as surely as any sharp blade.

CHAPTER 4

# Charles—and the Many Faces of Duty

*"The less people know about what is really going on, the easier it is to wield power and authority."*
*—Prince Charles*

Meghan's father-in-law will offer her a contrasting set of examples in how to be royal. First among them is that royal life is one of unremitting duty. On joining the Waleses' household, I quickly learned that what we courtiers *did* was our duty, and we had better do it to the very best of our ability. Or else. By contrast, for royal people, duty is not what they do—it is what they *live.* That goes a long way to understanding a royal person's view of the world and their place in it.

The key question for anyone finding themselves owner of a royal title is how best to discharge that duty, because any perceived sign of reluctance or ignorance where duty is concerned will eventually be noticed, if not by the subjects of the Crown then certainly by the ever-watchful media. In either case, the consequences can do great damage to royal reputations. A case in point: Harry's uncle Andrew, a younger brother who also built an admirable record of service to Queen and country, nevertheless lives with the burden of being nicknamed "Air Miles Andy," thanks to long-lens photos involving girls and yachts, insinuating a fondness for unearned foreign vacations.

We can assume that Meghan will be as eager as any princess in history to understand and fulfill all the requirements her daunting new position will impose on her. She has already announced that she wants to "hit the ground running." And it is a fact that being a British princess opens up uncountable opportunities to do valuable, satisfying, necessary, and just plain good works. It is a position that offers the possibility of unlimited personal fulfillment, fun, and happiness, made possible by resources both material and societal that eclipse anything achievable by the most acclaimed star of any screen, big or small. Just look at Grace Kelly—then multiply.

But ultimately, everything Meghan does in the course of her work, every cause she embraces (or declines to embrace), the company she keeps, the countries she visits, and every aspect of life on a *royal* red carpet, will be a matter for her own judgement. That especially applies to every word she speaks anywhere even slightly public from now on, since she must assume there's a mobile phone somewhere within earshot, faithfully recording every word. That can spell big trouble. She must also assume the same about paparazzi with telephoto lenses, and anyone with a mobile phone camera—though hopefully that's a risk with which she is already familiar from her own self-earned celebrity.

So we might imagine her studying the royal resumés of Prince Charles and Queen Elizabeth in search of a safe and uncontroversial track through what is potentially a reputation-killing minefield. And if Meghan has any doubts about the dangers that lurk off the safely trodden path of royal convention, there are plenty of cautionary examples for her to pick from.

As well as the reputation problems surrounding Uncle Andrew, she could also learn much from Harry's aunt Fergie (Sarah [Ferguson], Duchess of York), his uncle Edward—whose television career spelt disaster—and any number of ancestors. Comfortingly perhaps, it has been several centuries since any of her husband's forebears actually cut off the head of a wife who displeased him, but she should be in no doubt about the House of Windsor's ability and willingness to exercise some very modern tortures on errant newcomers.

Any survey of royal reputation management would highlight Prince Charles. Thanks to the efforts of co-operative biographers and a hard-working palace PR organization, progress has been made in portraying his second marriage as a national asset, enough probably to earn him and Camilla joint occupation of the throne on the day, which cannot be eternally delayed, when it becomes vacant. Yet it would be wise of Meghan to investigate, examine, and reflect carefully upon the causes and implementation of Harry's parents' divorce.

In doing so, her status as an objective foreigner, already unhappily wise to the pitfalls of an ill-starred marriage, should enable her to see past the mountains of words that have been expended on the subject, many of them intended to distort the reality. Among these must be counted the clumsy efforts of some misguided Charles loyalists to smear Diana not just as sad and mad, but bad as well. Others have been used to try to airbrush her out of the Windsor story altogether. As the Diana tragedy confirmed, when dealing with perceived threats, the Windsor dynasty—for all its modern associations with charity—can be quite uncompromising.

Meghan's new workplace has its own hazards. Whatever fairytale image she may have had of palace life, the reality is as old as time: behind the public image, courts are breeding grounds of intrigue, ambition, gossip, and jealousy. It's possible, of course, that in this they resemble some sections of the acting profession and so not entirely unfamiliar territory.

Harry's grandmother the Queen has demonstrated over the course of a lifetime in the public eye that modern constitutional monarchy works best when it sticks to the old rule "never complain, never explain." Meghan's father-in-law favors a different tactic, drawing criticism for what has been seen as an unwise amount of complaining, and an un-royal amount of explaining. Her absent mother-in-law, Diana, was also rather too fond of complaining and explaining although, in her defense, she might have learned the habit (like some other less-lovablc Windsor traits) from her husband.

Meghan may also observe that in a society as persistently stratified as England's, being a royal highness still attracts a surprising degree of deference. That combination of deference and unearned influence, amplified by sophisticated digital communication, probably represents the greatest threat to the future health of the monarchy.

Along with the hazards of unearned influence, Meghan may also want to watch out for its twin, the damaging effects of unearned praise. Royal people seldom actually personally *do* good work. Their job—and it's honorable and valuable—is to use their influence to draw attention to the good work of other people, who are usually less attractive, less wealthy, more dedicated, more hard-working, and generally more angelic than they are. Yet it is the royal person who collects the public recognition, and departs in a limousine laden with gratitude, flowers, and saintliness. Learning to derive worthwhile satisfaction from praise they have in reality done very little to earn is a valuable skill for royal charity champions. Otherwise, the danger of forming a false sense of one's own worth—good or bad—is very real.

As someone who surely needs no lessons in the performance arts, Meghan will understand the huge dramatic value of well-judged silence. Successful royal operators make full use of it, not least to motivate (i.e., terrify) courtiers. Royal body language also repays close study, if only because the media have their own experts who will be minutely analyzing hers.

Prince Charles is praised for his pioneering and committed work for many popular and important causes, from architecture and the environment to medicine and literature. And there will always be a core of loyal monarchists who will give him the benefit of every doubt just because he's going to be the next head of state. He is, after all, a man accustomed to being heard and to getting his own way.

Add those whose own sense of social standing depends on the preservation of a structure that has the monarchy at its head, as well as those who seek royal favor for their own agendas, and Charles has every reason to assume his long-delayed passage to the throne will be smoothly unobstructed. This despite the baggage he is carrying in the form of his second wife and former mistress who displaced Diana at his side.

So when the question is asked, "Will Camilla be Queen?" there are really only two answers. Supporters of Prince Charles, some establishment monarchists, and others who want to be in the new king's good books would probably say, "Why not?"

But those with a traditional model of royal propriety, or in whose memories and hearts the flame of Diana's memory still burns brightly, perhaps even including her children, would surely ask, "*Why*?"

This is a serious dilemma for those advising the monarchy on the traumatic challenge it must eventually face and which cannot be put off indefinitely: what will be the role of Camilla, Duchess of Cornwall, when Prince Charles becomes king? Anything less than Queen Consort will be seen by her lobbyists as not just a personal slight but a grave injustice to a woman who has endured so much opprobrium merely for the, as they would couch it, forgivable sin of loving an unhappily married Prince.

Intriguingly, in today's royal climate, where William and Harry and their wives and families now occupy center stage, theirs may be the casting vote on what happens to this elephant in the throne room. In that case, who can predict whether they would welcome the sight of the former Mrs. Parker Bowles enjoying the prize they may quite understandably feel had already been earned many times over by their mother?

Prince Charles has always seen himself as a modernizer, the reforming new broom that would sweep away the cobwebs on the throne he will inherit, many of them lovingly preserved since the days of Queen Victoria. Now in his seventies, the formerly young reformer can still be expected to leave his mark on the institution he has waited so long to head.

Ironically, for a dynasty that places so much value on its powers of youthful regeneration, Charles's successor as king will most likely be another elderly, bald white man, who, in turn, will most likely be replaced by another elderly, bald white man. This is not a product lineup calculated to appeal to a restless consumer society, especially as royalty indulges its habit of rubbing shoulders with surgically enhanced celebrities whose brands are rooted in youth appeal.

The only way to break this cycle would be for Charles to make way for William as next king, thus giving the crown a young family to represent it—as hasn't been the case for fifty years. Old kings are traditionally credited with the gift of grandfatherly wisdom; on the other hand, like King Lear, they may just as likely be self-pitying, cantankerous, and geriatric. By contrast, young kings, whatever their intellectual gifts or lack of them, have the unbeatable advantage in an image-obsessed age of being able to represent the experiences and aspirations of the people over whom they reign. They thus appear closer to and more representative of the country they lead, and more likely to be understood and forgiven when, inevitably, they fall short of the ideals they are supposed to embody.

Nobody seriously thinks that Prince Charles will pass up the opportunity to occupy and enjoy the throne he has spent his life preparing to inherit. Nor is there any sign that his wife would seriously prefer a life of obscure retirement, when the alternative is to share the pinnacle of honor and status in a country where many of the inhabitants still see her as an undeserving opportunist.[2] That being the case, the long-term health of the monarchy depends more than ever on William and Harry.

Had their parents managed to make a success of their marriage, this responsibility would still be far in their futures; instead, a media ever-hungry for royal material already treats them and their activities both in and out of the public eye as if they were the most important figures in the national shop window. And while, technically, the fate of the Windsor dynasty lies in the hands of William, Catherine, and their children, the watching world has been encouraged for many years to think of William and Harry as the eternally youthful duo who personify the royal future. So, inevitably, Harry will be seen as an integral part of the Windsor operation for the foreseeable future. This despite his diminishing constitutional relevance as William's children take precedence in line to the throne.

In this context, no wonder all eyes now turn to Meghan Markle—a divorced, American, mixed-race actress. Parallels with Edward VIII and Mrs. Simpson are

---

2 14 percent support Camilla becoming queen (YouGov poll, August 2017).

tempting but inaccurate, not least because Meghan can have no expectation of reigning alongside her husband. Nor is it conceivable that, as in the case of Edward or the unhappy Princess Margaret, the Prime Minister and Archbishop of Canterbury would combine to thwart the path of true royal love.

Interestingly, Harry and Meghan have the chance voluntarily to choose the option that was forced on the reluctant Edward of withdrawing from public life entirely and living as private citizens, with all the ease and opportunity their status and wealth could bring them. They could also say goodbye to the often-unwelcome responsibilities of maintaining a reputation for public good works, private decency, and selfless sacrifice.

If this were a tempting option, it's one they appear in no hurry to take, presumably out of a desire to fulfill a destiny of public service. It may yet be that the greatest service they will perform for the House of Windsor will be to retain the sympathetic support of youthful subjects, underwhelmed by the diminished promise of the next king and his wife.

CHAPTER 5

# William and Catherine and Harry…and Meghan

*"I think it's very important that you make your own decision about what you are. Therefore you're responsible for your actions, so you don't blame other people."*
*—Prince William*

Harry's marriage to Meghan supersedes the fraternal alliance that all his life has characterized his relationship with William. For many years it suited their father's spin doctors to portray the growing young men in a state of perpetual boyhood. This fitted a palace narrative in which they could be used as foils to manipulate media coverage of sensitive subjects, such as their stepmother's controversial elevation to royal acceptability, and their mother's consignment to a limbo where any discussion (or even celebration) of her life could conveniently be trashed as heartless.

Interestingly, the alliance with William is perceived as having been strengthened by the addition of Catherine, with the three joining forces in charitable activities and together neatly embodying the continuity of the monarchy, for example on ceremonial occasions when stylish Catherine nicely offsets the princes in their splendid military uniforms. At the same time, through initiatives such as the Heads Together mental health campaign, they have strengthened royalty's standing and relevance with the next generation.

Adding Meghan to the mix signals the end of this wholesome troika. In its place, a new entity has been created—a royal foursome uniting both brothers and their wives in an ambitious re-branding of the Windsors' traditional charity product.

Inevitably, it will suit some sections of the media to portray the two couples, particularly the two wives, as being in some kind of exclusive competition. Already, coverage is mixed about the latest shiny royal charity vehicle, some unconvinced observers detecting a tendency in the new American occupant to grab the wheel before she's learned which side of the road to drive on. Others think the arrival of a savvy, streetwise, self-made professional performer will give the whole machine a fresh new look and a welcome boost in horsepower.

This may not be the ideal long-term solution to the question of how to fit so many royal stars under one spotlight. Perhaps, as time passes and William's destiny draws him inescapably toward the throne, their paths will diverge naturally, with Harry and Meghan perpetuating the younger brother's traditional role as the irreverent but approachable and spontaneous inheritor of his mother's popular appeal, reinforced by Meghan's quickly established ability to charm crowds. This skill will also come in handy when dealing with any intimidating in-laws, and the old guard of courtiers who will be unfailingly friendly but will only rarely be her friends.

The simple fact that Meghan's family lives in America will add a whole new dimension to public perception of she and Harry as they are seen against the exciting new backdrop of her homeland. Whether intended or not, this will move them into a different category of royal celebrity; and while it has the potential to diversify and reinvigorate the entire royal brand, it also comes with an endless list of potential pitfalls.

Already one of the more intractable risks has added a note of unwelcome controversy to the royal romance. Speculation as to whether wedding invitations might be sent to presidents and former presidents, or one or the other, is a warning of the dangers involved in mixing cultures of celebrity and duty, America and Britain, the political with the strictly nonpolitical.

The instinctive duty of political neutrality is normally assumed to have been implanted in all royal people at birth. New royal people have to learn it—fast. In this instance, merely the suspicion that by their choice of guests Harry and Meghan have embarrassed the head of state of a key ally strikes at the heart of the principle that royalty is the servant of the national interest and the government of the day.

Princess Diana's popularity was rooted in the belief that what people saw was an accurate reflection of the woman she was. As I saw from my own observation over many years, the impression of a gutsy young woman doing her best to help those in need while simultaneously raising, as a single mother, two young sons *and* fulfilling exaggerated expectations as a royal role model was essentially accurate. Brand experts agree that authenticity is crucial not just to brand longevity but also to brand survival when, as it eventually always will, good news turns into bad and a reputational crisis strikes. That will be when enduring brands can call on deep reservoirs of public goodwill, when they can count on getting the benefit of the doubt; in other words, when they face an acid test of their "forgiveability."

The halo effect of Princess Diana has been inherited by her children. To their credit, they have also worked hard and with imagination to use their royal status for good and have enhanced it in the process. Keeping that hard-won reputation now depends on a benign public being willing to believe that the image of stylish duty that they project is a genuine portrayal of the kind of people they really are. For the younger Windsors to flourish, the public need to believe what they're being shown, must like it, want more of it, and be generous in their willingness to overlook any perceived failings.

Both William, Harry, and their advisers can take real satisfaction from the high trust ratings they have earned from a skeptical twenty-first-century media and public. But they must beware giving the impression of running a control-obsessed press operation, backed up by hungry lawyers on speed dial. If the public suspect that the attractive characters they see on screen aren't really as nice as they seem but are, in fact, the creation of clever news managers, the inclination to give them the benefit of the doubt—which one day they may desperately need—will quickly evaporate.

The era when newspapers had limitless budgets to pursue royal stories, when the royal narrative was marked equally by traumatic events and monstrous media scoops, is long gone. Now much of what appears in print or online about any member of the Royal Family has been supplied or sanctioned by a royal press officer. Thus in an ironic reversal, an ancient institution that commands visceral tribal loyalty from its followers is investing heavily in the latest techniques to present a digitally enhanced image of its true self.

This might work as a fair-weather strategy, but when the next major reputational crisis strikes the House of Windsor, it will be interesting to see if the thin skin of carefully spun digital perfection can withstand the sharp teeth of a media that has rediscovered the ability to bite the royal hand that has fed it such a homogenized diet for so long.

Until then, William and Harry will enjoy unprecedented freedom to determine how the public perceives them, their families, and the causes they choose to support. Their mother's enviable reputation as a legendary humanitarian was built in part on her willingness to get involved with unpopular and challenging issues such as AIDS, leprosy, addiction, domestic violence, and mental health, to name just a few. She drew enormous personal job satisfaction from being able to make a visible difference to these and other often neglected causes, while they, of course, benefited from their good fortune in attracting and retaining the most photogenic, engaged, and sought-after of all royal patrons.

The photogenic aspect was important: if the public could see in just a couple of glances the main elements of Diana's charity message then a consistent narrative would emerge, made all the stronger by being in picture form. After all, seeing is believing. Photos of Diana with a leprosy patient, walking in a minefield, or tenderly touching the cheek of an elderly refugee linger in the mind and reinforce the accurate impression of a woman devoted to her work and willing to take risks with her own safety to bring it to wider public attention.

I would always plan her visits wherever they were in the world in such a way that the questions "Why is she there?" and "What is she doing?" could easily be answered by the photographs that accompanied the story: the image of the beautiful princess in a variety of heart-tugging but thematically connected humanitarian contexts year by year created a story of dedicated service that sent powerful messages to friends and critics alike.

What's more, the acts of compassion recorded by the cameras, and the suggestion of many more where cameras were not present, bought the often-beleaguered Princess priceless amounts of public goodwill that seemed only to grow as her need for forgiveness and forbearance increased towards the end of her life.

For all her trademark spontaneity, however, Diana was extraordinarily professional and precise in her charity work. Every detail, from advance briefing material and thorough preparation on the ground to media, security, protocol, and punctuality, had to be strictly anticipated and faultlessly delivered. As I used to joke with her, "perfect spontaneity requires careful planning."

Central to the success of "Diana the humanitarian icon" was her own instinct for what made best use of her royal status and compassionate instincts, closely allied with a sixth sense for the media dimension. Thus she would veer away from causes that attracted valid public criticism (as opposed to those that merely attracted public ignorance) and concentrate instead on those that had a strong message that would resonate in the public mind. And if, coincidentally, they happened to provide an evocative backdrop for her own unsurpassed style of philanthropic work then that was a fringe benefit she was happy to accept.

Her sons and their wives have, of course, developed their own distinctive and admirable style of royal charity work. Harry, with his pioneering leadership of the Invictus games, has shown that he not only inherited his mother's people-pleasing approachability, but also her shrewd eye for a cause that can simultaneously meet an underserved need and, incidentally, reflect a golden glow on its royal patron.

Perhaps also taking a conscious leaf out of Diana's book, both her sons and Catherine have made highly publicized contributions to the destigmatization of mental illness, including a daring, and to some ears, overly candid confessional session in front of the cameras, during which they disclosed highly personal details of their own encounters with troubles of the mind. Arguably the success of this unprecedented delving into the contents of the royal mental attic was not helped by the carefully orchestrated publicity campaign that accompanied its delivery. Message control, when carried too far, kills the spontaneous authenticity that the younger Windsors have made their unique selling point USP. In this case it puts at risk a triumph of heartwarming princely accessibility.

One area where William and Harry have taken a very different tack from their mother is in their work to promote animal conservation, especially in Africa. While these issues may have irreproachable idealistic credentials and command their own distinct degree of urgent need, they transgress what for Diana was an iron principle, one that she instinctively understood connected her work with the experiences and priorities of ordinary people. Every year across my desk would come urgent and highly emotive pleas from animal charities, all implying a confident expectation that the Princess would follow widespread royal precedent in wishing to be photographed with an assortment of cuddly animals (in this they may have been influenced by the widely reported story that as a schoolgirl Diana was entrusted with care of the class guinea pig).

But their pleas all fell on deaf ears. With a response that spoke volumes for her own philosophy of how best to spend royal charity capital, she would say to me, "Patrick, we'll do animal charities when we run out of people charities!"

A similar policy from her sons would help safeguard them from the ever-present potential criticism that their interests and hobbies—which inevitably reflect their status as men of great wealth and privilege—should not overlap with their work as selfless servants of the public good. The damaging potential of this criticism is increased when set alongside William and Harry's stated desire to lead "normal" lives in which, presumably, they wish to be seen to be sharing the everyday concerns and anxieties of ordinary subjects. Their dedicated support for charities working with homeless people—to whom their mother introduced them when they were still boys—runs no such risks. In fact, it reinforces their credentials as in-touch princes more effectively than the most eloquent and smartly presented presentation on the evils of the international ivory trade ever could.

Success or failure as a prince, or princess, is most reliably left to the judgement of history. But in the age of relentless nonstop news, the considered assessment of years, even of centuries, is an unrealistic aspiration. It will be delivered eventually, but right now an enthralled constituency of royal watchers won't be able to resist closely following the perceived popularity ratings of individual Windsors.

By this measure, William and Harry and their advisors have good reason to feel satisfied: at an equivalent age, their mother was experiencing waves of international adoration, little of which translated into personal happiness. Worse, it was part of a toxic brew of royal dysfunction that saw their father vilified and their whole family mutate into an object of alternating pity and scorn.

Against that generation-old example, the princes' occasional media spats today are mere squalls in comparison to the constant hurricanes of the '80s and '90s. They and their advisors may have noticed, however, that one aspect of popularity has not changed—indeed, it probably hasn't changed substantially in centuries. In the world of red carpets, liveried footmen, and patrician courtiers, the price of public popularity can be a steep one. That's because, as Diana discovered, it was quite hard to make the watching Windsors share in and celebrate your success. And if you were seen to be hogging more than your fair share of scarce public approval, suspicious glances at garden parties and resentfully gritted teeth at state banquets could become the least of your worries.

Thus, in the constantly shifting power dynamics of the palace, a consistent record as a crowd-pleaser can be a distinctly double-edged sword. There are, however, some compensations for attracting icy gusts of jealousy from other members of the family, as Diana gradually came to realize. Commanding the persistent loyalty of significant sections of the country—let alone the watching world—delivers tangible returns in the form of hard-edged influence. Ever since the Stuart period, the British Royal Family has recognized the necessity to sniff the winds of public opinion and trim their sails accordingly. When this early warning instinct let them down (as with the Abdication crisis or their mishandled reaction to Diana's death) some last-minute sense of self-preservation kicked in, proving that pragmatism is a dynasty's most effective policy of last resort when survival is on the line.

How do William and Harry, and Catherine and Meghan score on the jealousy scale? We don't know, although a diligent study of media leaks from other royal households sometimes reveals the influence of the green-eyed monster. These are just petulant twitches, though, much easier to brush off than the full-blooded weaponized spin aimed at Diana. And any royal sabotage of the princes' reliably efficient reputation-management machinery would stand little chance against the alliance of sentimental fans and die-hard monarchists who stand ready to rush to their defense at the click of a mouse.

No wonder, then, that there's a suppressed fever of anxiety about what's shaping to be the constitutional flashpoint of the early twenty-first century. Camilla.

The former Mrs. Parker Bowles, known to Princess Diana in her more vengeful moods as "the Rottweiler," has been the beneficiary of one of the most skillful, sustained, lucky, and expensive personal reputation makeovers in the history of news management. The campaign to rehabilitate the future king's former mistress—to the point where she can, without serious opposition, expect to take the throne alongside her husband—is revered by some as a triumph of the spin doctor's art.

So keen were some of these unprincipled PR professionals to ingratiate themselves with their royal client that they even went so far as to concoct a quack diagnosis of mental illness with which they attempted to persuade the public that Diana was never really Princess of Wales material, let alone a viable queen-in-waiting. By deduction therefore, however unenthusiastic you might be about Camilla, at least she isn't nuts.

Throughout this campaign William and Harry were unscrupulously exploited as human shields—the most powerful potion in the spin doctor's cabinet—deployed to silence journalists who declined to toe the party line by writing Diana stories, thus keeping her memory alive despite dire warnings that their coverage would "upset the boys." What nobody ever seemed to ask was whether "the boys" might be even more upset that their father's advisers were systematically destroying the reputation of their mother in order to suppress public distaste for their stepmother.

William and Harry's own riposte to this demeaning and ultimately counterproductive campaign to write their mother out of the royal history books seems to have had to wait until they were grown men with independent royal careers, but it has been unmistakable in its main purpose. After years during which Diana's name was taboo in royal circles, thanks to her sons she is now a frequently remembered, integral part of their public and, we may assume, private lives.

From William's choice of his mother's engagement ring for his own bride, to the Princes' very public patronage of mental health charities and the erection of a statue to their late mother at Kensington Palace (incidentally her home as Princess of Wales and now the home chosen by her sons and their wives), the message to the Diana-deniers is clear: we share the public's affectionate memories of her, we are all inspired by her record of humanitarian public service, and hers will be a continuing guiding light for us as we adapt the institution of the monarchy to meet the challenges of the twenty-first century.

# Harry—Handle with Care

*"Conversations with my mother, father, my grandparents, as I've grown up have obviously driven me towards wanting to try and make a difference as much as possible."*
*—Prince Harry*

Royal life can be lonely. It's one of the ironies of a job that requires so much social contact that it also has the potential to be extraordinarily isolating. A large part of royal interaction, and especially that bit of it we see in public, is a kind of act. When I was at the palace we used to joke that nine-tenths of being royal was turning up at the right place at the right time in the right clothes with the right speech in your pocket and the right expression on your face. Not for nothing is the best advice any royal person might have is just to "smile and wave." It goes alongside "never complain, never explain" as one of the two great commandments of royal behavior.

To make the job even more isolating, much of it seems to involve accepting credit for other people's good deeds; how else can the royal patron of a great charity derive the essential job satisfaction and self-fulfillment that rank and file volunteers reasonably expect to receive from the simple dignity of their willingly-given labor?

This perhaps explains the ceaseless quest for "relevance" that has defined—and bedeviled—so much of Prince Charles's life and which we can also see motivating many of his sons' most reported and most commendable acts of public duty. There's a catch though. After a long day toiling in the royal quarry, royal performers do have access to enviable amounts of privacy and leisure time if they so choose; but I noticed that they could only ever really share the unique experience of their inherited destiny (Prince Charles is famously quoted as calling it "a predicament") with others who had also been assigned by fate to such a strange life, set apart from the rest of the human race.

Instead, in their day-to-day life both during and after working hours, their human companions tend to be either those on the royal payroll, from the most high-born courtiers to the reliably deferential junior domestics, or an assortment of hangers-on, many of them remarkable only for their talents as yes-men (and yes-women).

It's largely true that, as a royal person, the only source of effective discipline you may encounter is likely to be from yourself. Likewise, the only source of credible and useful approval, criticism, encouragement, or guidance is likely to be someone else with true blue royal blood in their veins. But even then, given royalty's intensified form of family politics and the tensions that can result, reliably honest and reassuring company can be very hard to find. How lucky, then, for William and Harry to discover that, from everything we can see, they each have in their brother a formidable ally, sparring partner, and confidant.

Siblings condemned to be motherless at an impressionable age can find in their brother or sister a lifelong soulmate, the only other person in the world who understands exactly how they are feeling. It's the kind of relationship that is hard to detect in what we see of Prince Charles and his younger brothers and sister; in fact, we would probably have to go back at least as far as the reign of George V to find a quality of brotherly love to compare with that which we see almost daily between Diana's children. Even better, and with truly good fortune, it seems to be a reliable structure of mutual support that extends to Catherine and Meghan too.

Closeness does not necessarily mean similarity. Even as little boys, William and Harry displayed clearly contrasting characters. William was the more conscious of appearances and the need to conform, while still harboring a streak of occasional willfulness that plainly wasn't easy to rein in. Harry, by contrast, never seemed to feel the weight of expectation that his mother told me was his brother's constant companion from the first day on which he comprehended the awesome responsibility that fate had in store for him.

As if to emphasize an instinctive recognition that his would be the more carefree while no less privileged life, he gleefully threw himself into testing every restraint that a concerned mother and relays of hard-working nannies could impose on him. It was said, with an indulgent smile, that if you wanted Harry to do something, the trick was to ask him to do the opposite. It was as if he was hardwired to be headstrong and contrary...which would be a pretty unattractive package had he not also been so winningly and, as a small boy, irresistibly forgivable. This rare gift was just one of many disarming talents he inherited from his mother, to a degree that even eclipsed his similarly blessed elder brother.

The stage was therefore set for Harry's teenage years to be packed with incident. The world that had watched with infinite sympathy the lost-looking little boy following his mother's funeral *cortège* (an experience, incidentally, that he later recalled as inhuman) was always going to be willing to give him the benefit of any doubt. Nevertheless, as he lost no time in proving, Harry seemed determined to put the world's forbearance to the test.

In a catalogue of misadventures that delighted editors of gossip sheets and tabloid Sunday newspapers, but drew exasperated grimaces from adherents to a more *bourgeois* form of staid royal upbringing, he seemed to take delight in seeking out boundary lines of acceptable behavior all the better to step recklessly over them. Memories of Harry wearing a Nazi uniform to a fancy-dress party—or wearing nothing at all while bingeing in a Las Vegas hotel suite—will take a long time to fade, even if the outrage they provoked—much of it synthetic—has happily dissipated.

These have been displaced by newer, more edifying stories of Harry the mature and plainly more evolved royal star. It comes as little surprise, but with considerable reassurance, that in more recent times a thoroughly grown-up Harry has spoken of those years as a time of miserable and directionless confusion. To his great credit, this realization and degree of self-knowledge is a feat that's probably rare among the fast living, self-indulgent, and privileged aristocratic crowd of which he naturally felt a part—and which seemed to have failed him when he was at his most vulnerable.

Another incident from those lost years is worth exploring in a little more detail, partly because of what it tells us about the temptations placed in front of teenaged Harry, and partly because of what it tells us of his father's high tolerance level for ethically dubious news management stratagems. In what was just one of many front-page scoops about Harry's out-of-control teenaged exploits, a Sunday newspaper gleefully reported that Harry and a group of like-minded friends were regular cannabis smokers. No doubt many of the concerned and even outraged public were reassured some days later by another story—in the authoritative *Times* of London, no less—that Harry's concerned father had arranged for him to visit a drug rehabilitation center where, while meeting staff and clientele, he learned a salutary lesson in the evils of illicit narcotics.

And there, perhaps, the story might have ended in a sober morality tale of a hard lesson well learned by a repentant Harry...had it not subsequently been revealed that the sequence of events described in *The Times* had been deliberately reversed by one of Charles's spin doctors. The cautionary visit to the drug clinic had actually happened *before* the dope smoking incident excitedly reported in the Sunday tabloid.

No wonder Harry found it hard to recognize that actions have consequences—or that bad news can't be magically dispelled by a little spin, revved up by courtiers anxious to burnish his father's credentials as a caring parent. Royalty's sometimes ambivalent acquaintance with the truth is unsurprising given their historic ability to organize facts in a way that matches their preferences. But it becomes even more dangerous when a modern generation of ambitious palace digital news managers is allowed to push the boundaries of what is ethically acceptable, in a great national institution that depends for its survival on public trust and goodwill.

Prince William's marriage to Kate Middleton in 2010 was not just the start of what is proving to be a reassuringly stable and visibly affectionate partnership, and thus a welcome return to the kind of solid middle-class values that were once the Windsors' trademark family style; it also marked the end of his status as world's most eligible bachelor, a title inherited by his younger brother for whom it seemed even more apt.

Harry's well-established and hard-earned reputation as a party animal and serial seeker after romance did nothing to diminish his eligibility, except perhaps in the eyes of nervous prospective fathers-in-law. Among a carousel of mostly blonde and aristocratic girlfriends, at least two, Chelsy Davy and Cressida Bonas, stayed the course better than most. Perhaps in the process, they gave a glimpse of Harry's willingness to seek, and even recognize the need for, a more permanent style of relationship. This desire to settle down, possibly spurred by his approaching thirtieth birthday, came just in time to reassure those, especially in the media, who were beginning to anticipate that the young prince's merry life would eventually attract harmful, even fatal, consequences.

An even higher chance of a fatal outcome was the risk Harry willingly took in pursuing his military career. The Iraq and Afghanistan conflicts of the late twentieth and early twenty-first centuries dramatically increased the combat casualty rate for young British Army officers. By forcefully expressing a desire to share the risks taken by others of his rank and professional training, Harry was following the example of his uncle Andrew, a Royal Navy helicopter pilot in the Falklands War, as well as that of his royal grandfather and great-grandfather, both of whom saw active service, including some of the most testing battles and campaigns of World Wars I and II.

Even so, it was horribly easy to imagine the propaganda value of a royal prisoner to an enemy such as the Taliban, were the fighting prince to fall into their hands. It was known that extra security was arranged for Harry to mitigate this risk, but the dangers he faced first as a forward air controller and then as an Apache attack helicopter gunner were still very real.

Harry was denied the prospect of returning to an operational theatre. With the demands of his military career increasingly incompatible with a growing workload of royal public duties Harry has now channeled his energies into an expanding portfolio of charitable causes, as well as the more routine round of public engagements and ceremonial that are the standard fare for all those in the upper echelons of the Royal Family.

With his grandmother the Queen and grandfather Prince Philip both starting to wind down lifetimes dedicated to an unrelenting schedule of official duties, the time was right for other members of the family firm, notably William and Harry, to increase their own work rate accordingly.

However, unlike aspects of military life, the role of a front-rank member of the ruling family is not rigidly structured by orders, routines, and clearly defined goals. Rather, the Windsors are like a business conglomerate, with the Queen equating to group CEO and subordinate family members running their own households rather like subsidiary companies, each enjoying a degree of autonomy that might surprise outsiders.

In the past, such freedom from central command and control has allowed the Queen's children the chance to develop their own individual royal careers and styles of operating their independent households. The cost has been a reluctance on the part of senior management to intervene in subordinate organizations, even when things are going badly wrong, as with the Wales subsidiary run by Charles and Diana. It was certainly my unhappy belief that early, energetic intervention from the head office would have imposed on the warring Waleses the clarity and resolve needed to reach a compromise that could have saved them, their family, and the nation an avoidable tragedy.

Harry and his brother have inherited this royal tradition of *laissez-faire* and with it the latitude to develop their unique royal identities. They have thus been able to explore their options for the kind of humanitarian work that not only brings credit to the institution of monarchy but also, we may hope, can give them a sense of fulfilment and job satisfaction as befits capable and energetic men in the prime of life.

For William this already includes the infinite joys and necessary skills of marriage and fatherhood, among them, we might guess, the art of compromise, which so regrettably seems to have passed his father by. Now it is Harry's turn to step into the constrained but also liberating world of married life.

In Harry's case, by contrast, whatever constraints he may feel at least do not include the daunting inevitability of kingship faced by his brother. Both princes and their wives might also cheerfully reflect that, unlike Charles and Diana, another generation must pass before they are required to assume the restrictions and responsibilities reserved for those at the top of the royal tree.

In these circumstances, Harry seems wisely to be playing to his strengths as a versatile, popular, and energetic royal operator, seen to be earning through hard work and his mother's empathetic touch with ordinary people, all the privileges that his status as prince-for-life undoubtedly bring him.

His effectiveness in this role has been proven in numerous philanthropic achievements, most notably the conspicuous international success of the Invictus games for disabled former service personnel. We might hope that these and other Harry-led contributions to British and international good causes will provide him with a lifetime's supply of inspiring challenges and professional fulfilment. We can hope, too, that for him and Meghan, life in the unforgiving spotlight of perpetual media fascination will remain blessedly free of the kind of marital straying and snares that precipitated his parents' bitter and horribly public divorce.

Significantly, his marriage to Meghan presents Harry with an opportunity to withdraw with dignity from the royal stage altogether and opt instead for the relative obscurity and normality of life as a private citizen. This was the course chosen by his aunt, the Princess Royal for her husbands and her children, and it was the choice imposed upon his great-great uncle King Edward VIII. Instead, after what we might hope was a sober process of careful consideration, Harry has committed himself and his bride to the strange demands and delights of a lifelong career as twenty-first-century inheritors of a thousand-year-old family business.

The royal firm may be grateful that they have retained his services as a diligent, telegenic, and congenial member of a hard-pressed royal workforce. The editors and proprietors of the world's newspapers and gossip magazines may be similarly relieved by the news. What only time will reveal, however, is whether Harry and Meghan made the right choice in offering up their lives to the unpredictable winds of public favor.

# “The Fab Four”– More than a Tribute Band

*“This is unity—at its finest.”*
*—Ms. Meghan Markle*

One of the great strengths of the House of Windsor is the freedom it has traditionally given its members to build their own successes—and occasional failures—in their own way. Since there is no centralized machinery issuing daily directives, a few guiding principles are considered sufficient to give royal apprentices all they need to know. The wisdom of this system is apparent in the quick success of The Royal Foundation, an umbrella organization set up to coordinate the charitable activities of Princes William and Harry, the Duchess of Cambridge (aka Kate), and, now, Meghan. Already dubbed "the Fab Four" by the British media, this group gives us a pretty clear idea of what the British royal operation of the future will look like.

The words chosen by Prince William to describe the broad objectives of the newly enlarged Foundation clearly underline that the two couples recognize the importance of maintaining continuity with the Royal Family's established charitable record:

"We would not seek quick wins but would strive to make a real and lasting difference.'"

He said they took inspiration from their parents, the Prince and Princess of Wales, who were "an example of diligence, compassion and duty," and their grandparents, the Queen and Duke of Edinburgh, who "had made support for charity central to their decades of service to the nation and the Commonwealth."

The very clear tribute to the previous two royal generations and to the Commonwealth, links senior Windsor management to the Foundation's activities, adding direction and legitimacy to its evolving mission. These activities continue work already begun by the Princes' parents and grandparents, thereby visibly reinforcing the continuity which is one of the Crown's principal constitutional functions.

They also revalidate royalty's unwritten pact with the people, that they will use their status and influence to benefit the monarch's subjects, especially those in greatest need. In this they connect with a theme largely pioneered by an earlier Princess of Wales, Alexandra of Denmark (1844–1925) a newcomer who channeled her misery at her husband's infidelity into a groundbreaking and often controversial new style of popular royal charity (sound familiar?).

It's part of this contract that royal people should be seen to pay for their lives of great privilege through hard work. How hard their work actually is might be open to debate since, unlike most people in their thirties, this Fab Four can largely determine their own schedules. This, combined with virtually unlimited resources and a high degree of privacy, means that any charitable burdens they choose to shoulder can be borne in reasonable comfort, the strain being further tempered by generous time allocation for holidays.

Nevertheless, the principle of privilege for sacrifice is one they would be wise to observe. A self-imposed curb on conspicuous consumption should be part of that wisdom, along with an unbreakable resolve never to complain about the unenviable toughness of their lot. In differently damaging ways, William and Harry's parents ignored that rule for their own short-term purposes, causing long-term harm to their children's inheritance. Along with "never complain," that other traditional royal maxim "never explain" could also usefully be adopted by the new generation as a time-proven defense against most forms of criticism.

Does this mean that William, Harry, Kate, and Meghan are just some kind of tribute band? There's plenty of evidence that while they may make full use of popular old material, they have the talent to create plenty of catchy new numbers as well. This corresponds with royalty's long-established habit of recycling proven themes in such a way that a new generation of fans needn't poke too hard at the glossy updated packaging.

Take, for example, the recent "Heads Together" mental health awareness campaign, which featured William, Harry, and Kate, who sportingly participate (complete with jokey headbands) in events intended to promote the destigmatization of this notoriously hidden affliction. This very professionally-packaged initiative is a direct extension of Charles and Diana's less-publicized work with mental health charities, from which it derives much of its legitimacy. Homelessness is another field in which William and Harry are paying tribute to their mother's work, with charities such as Centrepoint, by continuing a patronage that she started.

For Meghan, as with Kate, these charitable themes have no inherited resonance. After all, there can be few more compelling motivations than to carry on good work started by a much-missed and inspirational parent. So it makes sense for an incoming member of this formidable foursome to get rapidly acquainted with such a powerful guiding influence, even if its presence is largely unspoken. For motherless sons, their loss and its invisible touch on their decisions is not something they might necessarily feel requires discussion.

That doesn't mean William and Harry haven't generously shared their memories of their mother in the most affectionate terms with their wives. It may be, however, that such memories don't always come complete with practical, actionable tips for new princesses as they feel their way (despite every outward sign of confidence) onto an unfamiliar and very brightly lit new stage.

This may therefore be a useful opportunity to revisit aspects of Diana's royal career, taking an unsentimental look at some of her most- and least-successful experiences, and suggesting lessons and pointers that may be relevant to Meghan's new role. After all, coming onto the royal scene at the very age Diana was when she was taken from it, Meghan is already being cast as a form of continuation of the Diana phenomenon and will—voluntarily or otherwise—be compared by history with the mother-in-law she never knew.

Of course, there are hundreds of Diana books, articles, and television programs that a new royal princess might decide to study for useful examples and dire warnings. Or just as likely, she may choose to ignore all such dubious history, on the very reasonable grounds that she's about to make plenty of her own—and anyway, most of what's available is speculative or tiresomely adulatory or both.

But history—even dubious history—and the British Crown have a long, intertwined backstory that has always proved stubbornly relevant to unfolding events. That's unlikely to change now. What is offered here is based on my own front-row observation, so whatever value anybody may or may not place on it, it is at least the product of direct and sometimes painful experience.

With the emphasis already given to Meghan's non-royal ancestry (a subject that's unlikely to fade, given America's current obsession with tracing family trees) a good place to start would be Diana's surprising connections with the experiences of modern, very-unroyal working women.

Given Meghan's headline announcement that feminism will be a priority in her princess portfolio, this might very well be an area with which she can most readily identify.

It may come as a surprise to think that the impeccably aristocratic young Englishwoman, who stepped shyly into the royal limelight at just nineteen, could share any relevant common ground with today's female audience. All that high-class breeding, wealth, entitlement, access, and, there's no denying it, camera-friendly looks surely set Diana Spencer in a very exclusive bubble of inaccessible privilege. And all that is true. But look closer, and you may spot some more familiar touchpoints, especially as "Shy Di" began to find her feet and, sadly, lose her innocence in the daunting and even hostile world of palaces, red carpets, courtiers, footmen, and assorted in-laws, all long-term experts at what it takes to be a truly royal highness.

She quickly discovered, for example, that her role was largely decorative. As the wife of the heir, and therefore destined to be the next queen, hers was an essentially supporting function, delivering children (preferably at least one son) to prolong the dynasty. She was expected to look demure and attractively attentive when in public with her husband, and generally blend in invisibly with the deeply traditional, conservative, and ancient tableaux of royal life. (Ironically this organization, presided over by a female head of state, was—and largely remains—distinctly masculine in outlook and instincts.)

If Diana found she had time or inclination to look beyond these somewhat limiting parameters, she was expected to channel her energies into some suitable charitable patronage. A "suitable" charity could be assumed to be one that made little demand on her intellect or stamina (emotional or physical) and which kept her safely contained on the periphery of the circle of royal power.

Not that there was any malicious intent by those who assigned her these essentially superficial duties. Diana hadn't shown any intellectual aptitude at school and had hardly had time in the brief interval since to discover or develop any more visible talents, beyond being nice to look at and suitably deferential—except when showing some worrying signs of what was myopically interpreted as mental fragility. What else could those you might describe as her employers do, except maintain an outward show of happy normality while hoping for the best.

Meanwhile, essential help such as encouragement, guidance, patience, and some empathy were in conspicuously short supply, at least in any form that Diana recognized as being intended for her personal welfare. In its absence, what she perceived was intolerance towards any slip-ups on her part, and at best a condescending nod at any achievement she felt she had attained.

With all this taken into account, Diana's royal experience can now perhaps be seen as having substantial similarity to the frustrations and disappointments endured by many modern working women.

Consider:

- She lacked a network of supportive co-workers.
- Her superiors seemed distant and bound by a traditional code of behavior, remote from her needs.

- Her talents and abilities—what might be termed her professional potential—were either misidentified, underappreciated, neglected, or ultimately, resented and feared.
- Her achievements were marginalized while it seemed her shortcomings were exposed for all to see (sometimes in exaggerated form).
- Her unfaithful husband—and assigned mentor/professional superior—resented as competition any professional competence she developed, independence she showed, or acclaim she earned.
- Her private life lacked even the basics of moral or emotional support.
- Predictably, she felt betrayed by those she should have been able to look to for practical sympathy.
- Her attempts at protest were heard not with patient understanding but as proof that she had a defective personality.

...As a result of which, not altogether surprisingly, she struggled to overcome a persistent, debilitating eating disorder.

And yet, by her own efforts, she successfully devised and implemented a role for herself that recycled her own unhappiness to benefit those in need (especially the excluded or marginalized) and help reform the organization that had rejected her. In short, she "found her voice" and used it as one of many assets in her successful bid to be recognized as a strong and independent woman with a conspicuous contribution to make on a global stage.

She accomplished this in the face of a systematic campaign intended to undermine her personal equilibrium and public status, without surrendering an iota of her innate dignity or neglecting the respect owed to the throne that her son will one day inherit. This, and much more, she achieved while still younger than the current age of either of her daughters-in-law.

Such a record speaks volumes of Diana's determination not to be pushed aside, a determination that bordered on recklessness, especially when she perceived herself to be on the receiving end of injustice or disrespect. Perhaps what impressed me as her senior advisor and head of her whole public organization, was the degree to which her critics underestimated her strength and the instinctive emotional connection she made with ordinary people of every culture around the world.

This is an opportunity to explore in greater detail how Diana built a purpose for her life out of the stifling constraints of her early palace experience and the traumatic disintegration of her marriage.

In this context it's worth remembering that the sudden expansion of Diana's confidence and influence coincided with her discovery of an overseas role—as both diplomat at the request of the British foreign office and as charity super-ambassador. As time passed, she supplemented these primary roles with one-off personal trips (such as the one described in the opening chapter), which combined both charitable and personal agendas.

Being a foreigner already, Meghan has an advantage in establishing an international profile, previously used to great effect in her role with the United Nations. To this she can now add an almost infinite variety of Commonwealth-related duties, most of which will have the added benefit of reinforcing the organization's strong but largely undefined ties. As the time approaches for the Commonwealth to have a new head, any Windsor activity that assists both its survival and future relevance will be widely welcomed. There could be no quicker shortcut for Meghan to prove her value to a worldwide family of nations whose current and long-term potential has never been greater or more in need of recognition.

For Diana, the discovery of an international dimension to her work had to wait until after she had fulfilled an eight-year apprenticeship as the beautiful and dutiful appendage to her husband as he fulfilled a wide range of diplomatic, cultural, trade, and military obligations all over the planet. It was these early foreign trips that revealed some of Diana's future potential as a crowd-pleaser and as a formidable soft power asset.

Unfortunately it was the same positive qualities that increasingly revealed her husband's inability to demonstrate any real pleasure in her popularity and success. In other words, the seeds of future tragedy were visible to those with eyes to see from a very early stage. It did not take long for the honeymoon glow to flee Charles and Diana's marriage, to be replaced by a deepening chill of mutual mistrust, resentment, and suspicion—much of it well-founded.

Meghan and Harry have the advantage of close personal experience of the consequences of that rapid marital decline. They also have the advantage of being older, more experienced, and, we may assume, wiser than perhaps either of Harry's parents were when they started their partnership in royal public service. We might assume also that Meghan's previous journey from altar to divorce court has left markers from which she will find her way to a truly happy second marriage.

All of this bodes well for program planning sheets, filled with exotic destinations, each supplying their own photogenic backdrop to deserving causes, and heart-warming images of carefully choreographed spontaneous royal interaction with appreciative hosts. Palace press secretaries and editors of Sunday newspapers and glossy magazines can all share that special warm glow that only comes from seeing beautiful royal people behaving beautifully in beautiful locations. This is the essential glamorous counterpoint to the many hours of distinctly unglamorous work that also lies ahead for any conscientious royal couple.

Through it all however, especially when the pleasures and pressures of overseas representational travel are exerting their powerful influences, it's especially important to retain a firm understanding that such trips should never be confused with holidays, should never give the impression of frivolous expenditure of taxpayers' money, and least of all should never be used as platforms for the riding of pet personal hobby horses. When overseas, more than ever, any words that pass royal lips have the potential to cause far more harm than good.

Now would be an especially good time for Meghan to practice a highly desirable royal skill of seeing things as they are, not how one might wish them to be. Hopefully her advisers will find the right words to help achieve this essential clarity. Hopefully, in turn, she will develop a relationship with them which frees them from the risk of getting fired whenever they exercise this difficult but necessary part of their work.

Talking of advisers, Meghan will doubtless have valuable input on the subject of managing the small army of courtiers, officials, and junior staff whose job it will be to make her life as a Princess both enjoyable and successful. Special mention should be made of those employees whose jobs cover all the most menial tasks in the married household that she and Harry are now establishing.

Harry has the advantage of being born into a world in which staff and the money to pay for them were in plentiful supply. In his subsequent career in the British Army he will have found a reassuringly familiar pecking order in which everybody knows who is subordinate to whom and whose job it is to do the most onerous, repetitive, dirty, and usually thankless duties. Refreshingly however, not least thanks to his mother's influence, he clearly understands that his life would be impossible without such people and that they are to be treated with respect and consideration, the more so the more junior their position in his household. He has also shown that he has no problem rolling up his sleeves and doing such jobs himself if required. We even know that he was cooking a chicken in the very modest surroundings of Nottingham Cottage kitchen when he proposed to Meghan. Not something many of his princely ancestors could claim.

Alongside this well-bred concern for those at the bottom of the hierarchy will doubtless be a healthy realization that those drawn to the lowlier forms of royal service sometimes include those who take undue pleasure in seeing royal people at their least royal moments. The old saying "no man is a hero to his valet" is rooted in solid good sense: select and respect the domestic staff for their professional excellence, treat them well, and they will reward you with lifetimes of devotion that are humbling in their sincerity.

Meghan may have noticed, that old-fashioned notions of hierarchy are not necessarily evil hangovers from a heartless Victorian past. Treating your staff well is not to be taken as encouragement to be their friend. Royal friendships are notoriously fickle, and it does an employee no favors to extend to them the dubious honor of your secret confidences and generosity if these can be withdrawn at any time, to be replaced with some unspecified form of disapproval.

Meghan commendably says she wants women to have a voice and be heard; from the perspective of a subordinate, however, it is when your woman boss chooses to withhold her words that you know you're in trouble. A reliably stratified work environment—yes, that's all the bowing, curtseying, and "Your Royal Highnessing"—in which hard work is rewarded with honesty and good regular paychecks serves to protect the vulnerable and remind the powerful of their obligations to those who wash their dirty laundry (literally and figuratively).

In general, Princess Diana was an excellent boss who attracted a corresponding level of devotion from her staff both in the office and in all those behind-the-scenes places in palaces where the really hard chores get done. She would not have been human, however, if from time to time the pressures of her responsibilities didn't get the better of her judgement, not helped by the fact that as a single parent she was having to work twice as hard creating a safe and supportive environment for her family. Like many great people, she wasn't always easy to work for: she could be unpredictable, even capricious in her personnel management style and sometimes blurred the line between private and official business. But even on a bad day—and mercifully they were few—none of us was ever in any doubt that she was worth the very best we could give her.

Unlike Diana, however, Meghan can count on having a better-than-average chance of turning her marriage into the ideal foundation for a long, happy, and glorious life of service to the British Crown. An integral part of this fortunate partnership will be how she and Harry conduct themselves when representing the Sovereign, British foreign interests, British industry, the British armed forces, or any of their world-class charitable patronages. Her husband already knows the ropes in all of these potentially delicate areas of routine royal activity, and has earned for himself an enviable reputation as a royal operator of rare energy, empathy, spontaneity, and, when the situation calls for it, dignity.

Knowing instinctively when to function smoothly as a rock-solid couple, visibly pleased to be in each other's company, and when to stage carefully coordinated independent activity is a valuable royal skill. Like many such skills, its presence will hardly be noticed, but its absence will be pounced upon by an ever-watchful media.

In this context it was deeply reassuring at their official engagement photo-call to see so many clear signs of relaxed affection between Harry and his fiancée. Small, spontaneous gestures and an effortless frequency of eye contact were some of the little clues that helped decide the warm tone of media comment pieces that followed. It may not be fair, but it is certainly the reality that one of the best ways to ensure continued favorable media coverage for everything they do, will be for Harry and Meghan to treat the watching world to a regular supply of such nonverbal assurances that all is well in their marriage. And don't forget: every mobile telephone is a paparazzo waiting to snap a front-page jackpot.

Of all the skills Harry has already shown, especially in the overseas duties he has performed, probably the most important is appropriate dignity. He already has a well-earned reputation for the kind of lighthearted, unpracticed, and disarming informal interactions that can make people love royalty as well as just respect or even tolerate it. But what suits Harry doesn't necessarily translate to any other member of the Royal Family. Ultimately the watching world, friend and critic alike, will know if you are being yourself or if you are just acting.

Not that there's anything wrong with acting royal; often, it's an essential part of the job and the better the performance, the more widely it will be believed or at least respected. However, any suspicion that your public persona is not an honest reflection of your real personality will become obvious—sooner or later. And since for Meghan the royal career on which she is now embarking will last the rest of her life, it's wise to remember that almost nobody can keep up an act forever, so she might as well decide that the part of her that she allows us to see is both real and reliably predictable. Like a lot of things in royal life, honest continuity is more important than sparkling originality, clever lines or a constantly updated fashion sense.

One episode from Diana's experience draws all these lessons very neatly together. Before she and Prince Charles officially separated, we as their support organization devoted a huge amount of time and effort to suppressing rumors that their marriage was in deep trouble. In doing so, of course, we were suppressing the truth, a task that was both personally distasteful and organizationally highly corrosive. But we had no alternative, at least until the couple themselves reached a conclusion about what they were going to do to end the rapidly escalating speculation. Meanwhile royal life had to continue as normal.

This included the overseas program that, in the high summer of 1989, included a top-level diplomatic visit to Hungary, only just emerging from forty years of communist authoritarianism. In happier circumstances this would have been a perfect royal visit: there was real diplomatic purpose to our mission, the president and government officials, and the large crowds that everywhere turned out to see Charles and Diana were warm and welcoming; the Danube was blue in the sunshine, and Budapest was like the perfect setting of a Technicolor Disney movie. Even the Prince and Princess caught the mood and worked together in a way that poignantly reminded us that when they were on form they were a world-beating team. They may have been acting, but it was a good act and probably therefore consistent with any number of royal diplomatic successes over the centuries.

One incident right at the start of the visit didn't just score a personal PR triumph for Diana, it also underlined her extraordinary knack for expressing her genuine compassion in small acts of reliably consistent spontaneity.

The royal aircraft had landed precisely on schedule at Budapest Ferihegy airport. It slowed to a halt with millimeter accuracy so that when the door opened and the steps were deployed, the royal guests found the red carpet exactly where it should be (always a good start, I thought, from my perspective as one of the anxiously watching organizers). In the bright sunshine, the guard of honor crisply presented arms and while officers shouted their orders in an impressive display of military precision, the army brass band treated us to faultless renditions first of the British and then the Hungarian national anthems.

Everybody was hypnotized by the solemnity of the moment. Officers in uniform stood rigidly at the salute and the rest of us did a good imitation of statues, all eyes obediently looking at the ceremonial colors and the little group of motionless VIPs. Except one of the VIPs was not motionless. Princess Diana, using her formidable powers of observation, even out of the corner of her eye had noticed that the Hungarian president's wife—for whom this moment recalled the many years when her husband had languished as a political prisoner of the communists—had been overcome by emotion, and tears were silently streaming down her cheeks.

The rules of diplomatic protocol may have stipulated that we should all have remained motionless while the anthems were played, and the symbols of international friendship were properly observed in a moment of maximum secular reverence. But Princess Diana, who knew all the rules of protocol also knew when to break them. So she instinctively reached out a comforting hand, a gesture that the president's wife gratefully received. Which is why the lasting impression of that royal tour—not least for the watching Hungarian media—was of the tall, elegant figure of the young Princess holding hands with the no less elegant but visibly emotional First Lady of Hungary, a deeply touching and entirely human contrast to the stiff formality of the welcoming ceremony that carried on oblivious around them.

Such uncontrived spontaneous evidence of the Princess's natural compassion and of her willingness gently to flout the rules in order to express it offers a master class in effective use of royal soft power. Much of its potency came from the realization that the Princess was not ignorant of the rules of diplomatic protocol, quite the reverse, but she knew when to break them and had the confidence to do so.

It was the same instinct and confidence that was the hallmark of her most effective humanitarian influence. Picking up an African baby dying of AIDS. Sitting with a group of homeless drug addicts. Joining a meeting of the patients' council at a hospital for the criminally insane. Comforting a dying refugee in a wintry Balkan transit camp. Hugging a leper. These were not the actions of an emotionally inadequate actress, or a grandstanding do-gooder posing for the cameras. Instead, these were the unrehearsed responses of a woman seeking the most effective way to use her extraordinary international public profile to comfort people with whom she felt an instinctive affinity.

Beyond the most elementary logistics, they had not been set up by her handlers; very often they were entirely hidden from the cameras. Sometimes they inadvertently triggered distracting consequences, such as when she innocently strayed onto the territory of pre-election political controversy over policy on homelessness. Yet even then, her critics made allowance for her irreproachable motives and genuine compassion. In short, she was given the benefit of the doubt, over and over again.

What celebrity, what commercial brand, what politician wouldn't give their right arm for such forgiveability?

People liked what they saw, believed it to be authentic, and wanted more of it.

This may be an unrealistically high bar for any royal newcomer to be expected to clear. This may also be why suggestions that Meghan may be the new Diana are, at least for now, well wide of the mark. Yet forgiveability, through honesty and sustained, low-key hard work can be earned even by the majority of us unblessed by the gifts with which Diana was born. Indeed, for any royal operator, newcomer or veteran, building up sufficient reserves of public goodwill may very well be the House of Windsor's best guarantee of long-term survival.

CHAPTER 9

# The Meghan Factor Meets the Majesty Factor

*"There is not a single crowned head in Europe whose talents or merit would entitle him to be elected a vestryman by the people of any parish in America."*
*—Thomas Jefferson*

As we celebrate a royal wedding, it's worth remembering how such human family events serve to mark the passage of time for the Windsors. Unlike an elected head of state, a British sovereign knows he or she will never have to face the voters to remain in office. Not for them the constitutionally set intervals at which the people's opinion must be sought, or the seemingly endless campaigning that roils the modern political scene.

Their reign—like all the reigns before them in history—has a length known only to God and He, in His own good time, will decide when there needs to be a change at the top. Nor is the divine reference accidental: after all, the king or queen of England is also Head and Supreme Governor of the Church of England, an ecclesiastical leader who inherits the status won when Henry VIII split from Rome. A coronation, unlike a presidential inauguration, is an overtly religious event, the crowning forming part of Holy Communion. The idea that the fortunes of the British monarchy are under a watchful heavenly eye is not a religious fantasy or even a product of faith: it is the official belief of monarch, church, and state.

Not all reigns ended with the death of the incumbent. In a handful of cases, the Almighty might be seen to have acted through human activity to sack an unsuitable king. As we have seen, this was the fate of Charles I and James II when their subjects, acting through

Parliament and sections of the aristocracy, risked their own necks in the cause of limiting royal power (my own ancestor, William Jephson, among them, incidentally).

And then there was Edward VIII—"half child, half genius" in the words of Prime Minister Stanley Baldwin. The King's intended marriage to Wallis Simpson was deemed to put the monarchy at risk and so, despite opposition from Winston Churchill among others, he was driven—politely but very firmly—into exile in 1936. He took with him the American divorcee who precipitated the crisis and with whom he lived out the rest of his life cut off from his homeland and family, to say nothing of all the pomp and circumstance that, as king, would have been his by right.

In his place, the throne was passed to his reluctant, stammering brother George VI. It was this diffident and dutiful man who quietly inspired the British Empire to endure and triumph in World War II, and who then bequeathed to his country the unsurpassed and mercifully still-continuing blessing of his daughter Elizabeth's reign, currently the longest in history. It's synchronized history like this that might persuade the most reluctant believer that the House of Windsor has a direct line to the King of Kings.

Early in Elizabeth's reign she faced a constitutional crisis over her sister Margaret's choice of intended husband, a divorced war hero. As crises go, it didn't rank with Edward VIII's abdication, but on a personal scale the shared hurt and family trauma must have been extreme. In what now looks like a quaint medieval-style act of religious piety, Margaret sacrificed her own hopes of happiness in obedience to the Windsors' commitment to uphold the teachings of the Church, which forbade remarriage of divorcees. She subsequently married—and in due time scandalously divorced— society photographer Antony Armstrong-Jones, who passed the Church test.

While these events were in the distant past, and, since Meghan's arrival, seem even further, they remain relevant, and not just because another American divorcee is shaping to marry into the world's most famous family. The Abdication Crisis is recent family history so far as the Windsors are concerned, given their uniquely unconstrained sense of the passage of time. It occurred in the current queen's lifetime and, along with the stresses of her sister's canceled wedding plans, must linger among more recent memories.

More stresses were to follow. In quick succession, the marriages of her daughter, her second son, and finally her eldest son one by one came very publicly, painfully, and messily to grief. Meghan may have done the arithmetic. It's rather sobering: in the past sixty years there have been six church weddings of first-rank members of the Royal Family. Only two survive. That's a failure rate of nearly 70 percent.

Surely that doesn't matter? Every case is different, Meghan and Harry are fully evolved, experienced, and definitely adult people, entering into a lifetime's commitment with no illusions but, quite obviously, an enduring love for each other, buttressed by a wealth of shared philanthropic interests. Don't try to rain on their parade with doleful stories of past mistakes!

And so we probably shouldn't. But somewhere, deep in a palace, on some red-carpeted corridor where dedicated courtiers labor in their offices to ensure that the Windsors live long and prosper, somebody must have recognized the potential for the Meghan effect to cause an earthquake to rank with any that have shaken the monarchy in recent years.

This might be a good moment to examine in more detail the last serious earthquake to rumble its way through the sometimes-wobbly foundations of the House of Windsor. It's relevant because it illustrates the consequences of a failure of marriage-management—a failure that we might assume a pragmatic Meghan has studied in some detail.

It was the summer of 1992 and I was driving from Charles and Diana's residence at Kensington Palace to their then still-united office in St James's Palace (just across the road from Buckingham Palace)—a journey that I could usually manage in twenty minutes, sometimes less if the London traffic cooperated. The drive was one I sometimes had to make several times a day, a tedious and often stressful chore in a work schedule that was already very well stocked with worrying things for the Princess's private secretary (me) to fret over. Coincidentally, I was about the age Meghan is now.

The journey may have been a nuisance, but it also gave me valuable time to think, on my own and away from the uneasy palace atmosphere. As usual, I was thinking hard about what could possibly resolve the intractable problem of Charles and Diana's marriage that was daily disintegrating in front of our eyes and yet which we were still trying to sell to the outside world as a viable proposition. It was a horrible dead-end for us advisers (much worse for them, of course) with no way out that we could see since divorce—even a separation—was out of the question.

There had never been a divorced Prince of Wales before, and we courtiers definitely liked to follow precedent. Just think of the constitutional implications, William and Harry, the PR disaster, the Church...the list went on and on. Divorce was a non-starter. We had already considered every alternative we could think of, including—in desperation—a reprise of the Edwardian version of an open marriage in which the husband and wife lead effectively separate lives but are able to bear each other's presence long enough to put up a convincing show of togetherness in public. But as we had seen on too many occasions, Charles and Diana weren't in a mood for such playacting.

I was just approaching Hyde Park Corner, an intimidating, high-speed traffic interchange in the middle of London that was a challenge even when my mind was undistracted by imminent constitutional crises, when my mobile phone rang. It would be illegal now but in those days it was sort of okay to phone and drive so, swerving only slightly, I picked up the handset and immediately found myself talking to my boss.

"Patrick!" she said, sounding very calm and deliberate. "The Prince and I have decided to separate."

I swerved a lot more this time, earning a long blast on someone's horn. But the relief was instant and overwhelming: this might be terrible news on every level, and it certainly was taking us into uncharted constitutional territory. But it was better than the ghastly dead-end we were stuck in. Now at last we could stop pretending and instead deal with the reality of the situation, however unpalatable.

"Good," I said. And meant it.

Before long, I found myself fighting her corner in an extraordinarily intense two weeks in which I worked with my opposite number on Charles's staff to hammer out some form of agreement that would satisfy our bosses' requirements, while also addressing what seemed like thousands of questions that were the fallout from such an unprecedented development. We were helped by members of the Queen's private office and press office and by an expanding circle of experts: from Downing Street, Lambeth Palace (the Archbishop of Canterbury's office), specialists from our own household and, inevitably, lawyers. And all our work, every conversation and hypothetical possibility—even the mere fact that we were holding meetings—had to be kept strictly secret.

As you can imagine, it was an incredibly tense process and also a heavy-hearted one. After all, despite Charles and Diana's differences and the prickly fault lines that were developing in our own office, these were people we knew well, talked with every day, and shared all the closeness of an isolated professional existence. Nor were concerned thoughts for William and Harry far from our minds.

We labored with quiet intensity in the St James's Palace conference room, on whose walls hung portraits of great Britons from times gone by. They seemed to stare down at us with disapproving eyes. Outside the tall windows, past the white net curtains, the outside world carried on oblivious, although some of the press were beginning to scent trouble and a storm of speculation soon began to rage around our little oasis of grimly focused calm.

As the days passed, I increasingly lamented to myself that if we had put the same level of effort into keeping our bosses together as we were now devoting to splitting them up, we might not have gotten into this mess in the first place. If we had been able to conquer our instinctive reflex to deny bad news, keep up a façade of business as usual and hope for the best, we might instead have had some chance of finding workable alternatives to the irreversibility of separation. But we had missed those chances and so here we were performing the last rites on a marriage that had started with such hope, on a wave of worldwide goodwill.

All that remained was for Prime Minister John Major to announce to a hushed Parliament, on December 9, 1992, that the Prince and Princess of Wales were to separate, and that there was no reason why Diana should still not be queen. (I was quite proud of that, though it certainly raised a few eyebrows.) Although the divorce took several more years to become absolute, the marriage effectively ended then.

Both Meghan and Harry have had to live through more than their fair share of disrupted family life. Both come from what used to be called broken homes, and Meghan has since had firsthand experience of terminating a troubled marriage. It's safe to assume that they are under no illusions that life together in the public eye is going to be an endless bed of roses. Fortunately, anyone who has seen them together can tell that the obvious affection they show for each other is very much The Real Thing. And when, as they very probably will, the ordinary challenges of married life seem to descend on them in daunting numbers, they will have the personal resources necessary to get through the toughest problems, and always find their way back to the mutually supporting closeness that we already see.

From my own experience as Princess Diana's senior official advisor at the time of her separation, I suspect some of the greatest challenges will be faced by the staff whom Harry and Meghan choose to support them. The task of staying focused on events as they are not how they might wish them to be, puts a special obligation on their staff to discount everything except the cold hard truth when offering their considered opinion. Of course, the best, most clear-eyed advice is useless if it isn't delivered in ways that make it possible for the royal recipient to act upon it. But then, that's a skill Harry and Meghan's courtiers have already mastered. And they'll have to keep mastering it.

♛♛♛

So is it an exaggeration to describe Meghan's impending arrival on the balcony of Buckingham Palace as a potential earthquake? Not if you recognize that the

Windsors, for all their impressive titles, crown jewels, castles, palaces, estates, artwork, bodyguards, helicopters, and armies of staff, are actually surprisingly insecure. Perhaps it's because they know that almost all these trappings on which their special status depends are held in trust for the people over whom they have been set. Even the assets they might be entitled to call their own could be seen as fortuitously acquired rather than earned.

The knowledge, even subconscious, that all these tangible indicators of their royalness could be taken away or, almost as bad, carelessly lost through miscalculation, would shake the self-belief of a dynasty even as outwardly self-assured as this one. It's worth noting that one of the very rare occasions on which Elizabeth II was seen to shed a tear in public was at the decommissioning of the Royal Yacht *Britannia*, a royal asset of unsurpassed elegance and charisma, axed by the Ministry of Defence as a cost-saving measure.

Add the amplifying effects of a modern news media whose pliability must constantly be repurchased through a complex system of trades and favors, and then add the online anarchy of social media that picks the scab off every rumor and defies any traditional form of control. Pretty soon the survival odds for the world's last remaining major monarchy begin to look rather less impregnable.

Then add the unimaginable tectonic shift that will follow the not-far-distant end of Elizabeth's reign, followed by the no less unsettling implications of the coronation of King Charles and Queen Camilla, and the odds look shakier still.

Meghan and Harry may, in constitutional terms, be strictly irrelevant. They will never ascend the throne and their public function, insofar as they have one at all, is to support the crown...and avoid bringing it into disrepute. It's a delicate structure—a democratic monarchy that has taken centuries to reach its current, finely-balanced state of broad public approval. For Meghan and Harry everything else, even developing a globally acclaimed portfolio of irreproachably good causes, is superfluous.

That's not to say that earning a reputation as a selfless, inspirational royal Mother Teresa-figure would be a waste of time. The warm-glow effect of public good works has long been recognized as valuable evidence of royalty's fundamental worth, whatever their day-to-day missteps. Presumably, that's why the decision was taken to bind Meghan and Harry into the "Fab Four" grouping of the Royal Foundation, alongside William and Kate.

This might even be seen as an act of generosity by William, whose royal destiny is very different from that of his brother. In fact, protection of that destiny might have argued for using Meghan's arrival as an opportunity to spin off the junior members of the band, preserving for William and his fast-growing children the option of a closely controlled charitable repertoire that kept to the safety of the middle of the road. After all, monarchs are seldom executed for being boring.

High-profile support of uncontroversial causes will see them through the lean times of public disapproval and a reputation for consistent, low-key hard work will definitely help when the cost of royal jets/holidays/protection officers and all the other perks is being debated in Parliament and in the media.

It's at that moment that royal people's avoidance of controversy can be their lifesaver. Because if they have unwisely taken positions on matters of public policy—especially if in doing so they have caused or deepened public discord—then they will have betrayed their primary constitutional function, which is to act as a non-political focus of national unity. They will thus have undermined the very purpose for which they exist and in return for which they are allowed to live lives of such privilege and influence.

In other words, for a minor royal figure to undertake very few charitable engagements might not do the House of Windsor very much good but, beyond a little media grumbling, won't cause it irreparable harm either. But think of the alternative: the same could definitely not be said if he or she championed causes that, whatever their ostensible good intentions, were believed to inflame national divisions.

Bottom line: the monarch aside, it is no part of royalty's remit to save the world or anything in it. Or preach at us, or admonish us, or signal any fashionable virtue. Their job is to exist, preferably without rocking the constitutional boat. And if in the process, by the way they lead their own lives, they gently inspire us to do more and better with our own, then they will probably be treated with respect and remembered with affection, far into the future.

Meanwhile…#CoolIt. You have all the time in the world.

# Epilogue

It's 2040, and King Charles (ninety-two) has been on the Throne for ten years—though somehow it feels far longer. Prince William (fifty-nine) and Prince Harry (fifty-seven) have been inexorably eclipsed by their children in public fascination and affection. Like their father, and many of their male ancestors, they live in the shadow of their wives. That's because, as so often was in the twentieth century, it's the Windsor women who have kept the show on the road, especially in the bad times. Perhaps, despite all the banana skins of a marriage lived in the spotlight, choosing an actress with smiling eyes was the best and cleverest thing Harry ever did.

Even after all these years, that happy thought is still uppermost in his mind almost every day. *Especially* today, as he proudly walks his strikingly beautiful daughter up the aisle. She's the very image of her mother. And look, among the lucky wedding guests in Westminster Abbey, isn't that the first woman president of the United States, Ivanka Trump...?

# About the Author

Patrick Jephson was Princess Diana's equerry chief of staff 1988–96 and is also an award-winning journalist, broadcaster, and bestselling author. Now a U.S. citizen, he is a brand and reputation consultant in Washington, D.C. His first book, *Shadows of a Princess*, was hailed as "the most indelible and authentic portrait" of the world's favorite princess.

Printed in Great Britain
by Amazon